The
Healthy Hound
COOKBOOK

Over 125 Easy Recipes for Healthy, Homemade Dog Food—
Including Grain-Free, Paleo, and Raw Recipes!

Paris Permenter and *John Bigley*
DogTipper.com

Aadamsmedia
Avon, Massachusetts

Published by
Adams Media, a division of F+W Media, Inc.
57 Littlefield Street, Avon, MA 02322. U.S.A.
www.adamsmedia.com

ISBN 10: 1-4405-7282-8
ISBN 13: 978-1-4405-7282-1
eISBN 10: 1-4405-7283-6
eISBN 13: 978-1-4405-7283-8

Printed in the United States of America.

10 9 8 7 6 5 4 3 2 1

Library of Congress Cataloging-in-Publication Data

Permenter, Paris, author.
  The healthy hound cookbook / Paris Permenter and John Bigley, DogTipper.com.
    pages cm
  Includes index.
  ISBN-13: 978-1-4405-7282-1 (pb)
  ISBN-10: 1-4405-7282-8 (pb)
  ISBN-13: 978-1-4405-7283-8 (ebook)
  ISBN-10: 1-4405-7283-6 (ebook)
  1. Dogs--Food--Recipes I. Bigley, John, author. II. Title.
  SF427.4.P47 2014
  636.7'085--dc23
                    2013051347

Many of the designations used by manufacturers and sellers to distinguish their product are claimed as trademarks. Where those designations appear in this book and F+W Media, Inc. was aware of a trademark claim, the designations have been printed with initial capital letters.

Always follow safety and commonsense cooking protocol while using kitchen utensils, operating ovens and stoves, and handling uncooked food. If children are assisting in the preparation of any recipe, they should always be supervised by an adult.

This book is intended as general information only, and should not be used to diagnose or treat any health condition. In light of the complex, individual, and specific nature of health problems, this book is not intended to replace professional medical advice. The ideas, procedures, and suggestions in this book are intended to supplement, not replace, the advice of a trained medical professional. Consult your physician before adopting any of the suggestions in this book, as well as about any condition that may require diagnosis or medical attention. The author and publisher disclaim any liability arising directly or indirectly from the use of this book.

Cover design by Frank Rivera.
Cover image © Adams Media.
Photography by Elisabeth Lariviere.

This book is available at quantity discounts for bulk purchases.
For information, please call 1-800-289-0963.

DEDICATION

To our Irie and Tiki, our hard-working taste testers!

Acknowledgments

A huge thank you goes to the readers of DogTipper.com and their dogs. We surveyed our Facebook and Twitter communities about their dogs' likes and dislikes in terms of meats, fruits, and vegetables. Their input was an enormous help in the formulation of these recipes.

And another round of thanks goes to our blogger friends, ones who through the years have helped us spread the word on everything from our latest projects to adoptable dogs. They share our love of furry, four-legged family members and all that makes them special.

Contents

Introduction

Greetings, fellow dog lovers, and welcome to our kitchen! Like you, we are pet parents who share our lives with our furry family members—and that includes cooking the occasional meal or treat for them. Using whole foods, we enjoy whipping up dishes for our dogs Irie and Tiki—including many meals that we all share.

Whether you would like to prepare Sunday doggie dinners, the occasional special celebratory meal, or everyday dog treats, it's easy to do—and it's always very appreciated!

This book is also perfect for pet parents who want to take the leash in terms of their dog's diet. Maybe you want to avoid giving your dogs all the preservatives and additives found in many store-bought dog treats. Perhaps you love cooking and want to offer your dog foods made with in-season produce that's packed with nutritional value. Or maybe your dog needs a particular specialty diet that's costly to purchase. Just as there is no single best diet for every person, there isn't one diet that's best for *all* dogs. Every dog is an individual—some will thrive on one diet, while others do best on another. Many pet parents want to feed their dogs a wholesome specialty diet. No matter what type of diet your dog needs—from grain-free to Paleo to raw to traditional—you'll find recipe examples in this cookbook. Just look for the icons (GF P R) for easy reference. Choosing the best diet for your dog is a job that you should take on with the help of your veterinarian to determine the best foods for your dog's breed, energy level, and life stage.

Unlike cats, who are obligate carnivores and need a diet primarily consisting of meat, dogs eat (and enjoy!) a varied diet. As you can tell from your dog's teeth, which are meant to tear, but not chew and grind, the canine diet naturally leans heavily toward meat, too, but dogs can also digest and savor many fruits and vegetables. Fruits like bananas, blueberries, blackberries, and more will provide a tasty addition to your dog's treats and meals while serving up great nutrition as well. And don't forget veggies! From asparagus to zucchini, dogs love fresh vegetables. We'll provide recipes for many seasonal favorites like sweet potato and pumpkin; you'll also find many recipes that provide a template for using your own dog's favorite veggies depending on the time of year.

This book introduces you to the many wholesome foods that you can be proud to serve to your best friends. You'll help them enjoy their meals and treats, and live healthy lives, too.

CHAPTER 1

Why Homemade?

While there are many high-quality commercial dog foods available in stores these days, many dog lovers like to prepare at least the occasional meal and treats at home. We find that cooking for our dogs is rewarding for us as well. When we watch them enjoying a meal we have prepared especially for them, we feel satisfaction at having created something our dogs love, and their eager eating proves that they appreciate it.

CONTROL OVER INGREDIENTS AND QUALITY

Aside from the sheer "joy of cooking," probably the biggest advantage of homemade dog foods and treats is having control over exactly what your dog is eating. By choosing fresh ingredients and preparing them in your own kitchen, you are free of the worries of byproducts, fillers, and recalled foods and treats. You'll be making canine cuisine from ingredients you've purchased and prepared, just like you do for foods for every other member of your family.

In 2007, many dog foods were found to be tainted with the industrial chemical melamine—causing the sickness and tragic deaths of many animals. The event drew the attention of so many dog lovers, and for the first time, many people began to look closely at the ingredients list of their dog's treats. Many pet parents opted to buy only U.S.A.-made treats (the melamine was linked to ingredients imported from China), while others decided to head to their own kitchens to prepare nutritious homemade treats using whole foods. Not only is making your own treats a way to use ingredients you know and trust, it also a great way to share your love with your dog.

Also, control over your dog's diet means that you are more actively invested in his nutritional health, keeping you on your toes as far as the quality (and quantity) of the food you feed, rather than simply following feeding recommendations on the back of a bag.

EMPHASIS ON SEASONAL VEGETABLES AND FRUITS

Hand in hand with being able to choose your own ingredients is the benefit of selecting fruits and vegetables during their peak season—a time when they're not only less expensive, but also more nutritious. Fresh fruits and vegetables provide excellent nutrition for your dog. While dogs' digestive systems cannot break down the cellulose walls in raw plant cells, they *can* utilize these nutrient-dense foods when you cook them or you break them down in a juicer, blender, or food processor. Those all-important nutrients are bio-available to your dog after you purée, juice, steam, or cook that fruit or vegetable.

Which fruits and veggies are good for your dog? As with people, the brightly colored vegetables and fruits are some of the most nutritious. Some of our favorites to incorporate in our dogs' meals include:

- **Green beans:** A great source of vitamin A, green beans are also a wonderful way to help your hungry hound feel full without packing on the calories. If you don't have fresh green beans, canned will work, but look for a low-sodium variety.

- **Pumpkin:** Pumpkin is not just a fall favorite (when we buy it fresh, purée it, and freeze it for later use—it'll keep for a few months); it can be a great choice for dogs year-round. Amazingly, pumpkin can be helpful for both constipation and diarrhea, and it's also another excellent food for making your dog feel full. If you don't have fresh pumpkin, you can purchase canned pumpkin purée (but not pumpkin pie filling, which contains sugar and spices).

- **Carrots:** Carrots are a favorite snack for many dogs, enjoyed raw as an alternative to a rawhide chew. For your dog to get the nutrients in the carrot, though, you'll need to steam, cook, or purée the carrot to unleash its powerhouse of vitamins, such as vitamin A and beta carotene.

- **Sweet potatoes:** Like carrots, sweet potatoes make a great chew (see our recipe for dehydrated chews in Chapter 7), but you can also purée them and add to any meal for a great source of vitamin E as well as vitamin B$_6$, vitamin C, beta carotene, and more.

- **Blueberries:** Rich in antioxidants, this superfood is a favorite with many dogs, ours included. You can include them in a meal, serve them separately as a little treat, and freeze them for some added crunch.

- **Eggs:** Not only are eggs an economical source of protein for your dog, but they pack a real punch in terms of nutrients. You'll find numerous recipes for egg dishes and treats in this book. Some proponents of raw diets also favor feeding eggs raw. However, be aware of two potential issues: food poisoning from salmonella or E. coli, and the presence of avidin, a vitamin B inhibitor that's found in uncooked egg whites. If you feed uncooked eggs regularly, just be sure to feed the entire egg, not just the egg white.

- **Peanut butter:** Dogs love peanut butter, and it's an excellent source of protein as well as healthy fats and vitamins. Look for natural peanut butter without added sugar (and organic, if possible).

- **Spinach:** Our dogs enjoy salads, but spinach can be served in many ways that effectively deliver the iron that's found in this leafy green.

- **Bananas:** Bowsers and bananas go hand in hand (and add in a little peanut butter and you'll be a gourmet in your dog's eyes). That banana is also packed with nutritional goodies, including amino acids, electrolytes, minerals, vitamins B6 and C, potassium, fiber, and manganese.

Along with fresh versions of favorite fruits and vegetables, don't discount frozen varieties either. Many frozen foods are picked at the height of freshness (unlike veggies in your market, which may have been picked before ripening so that they ripened in transit to the store). Frozen vegetables and fruits can be a great way to stock up, enjoy out-of-season produce, and save some preparation time in your cooking.

ABILITY TO CATER TO SPECIALTY DIETS

This book includes traditional meals and foods as well as recipes that work for several special diets: grain-free, Paleo, and raw. Following are some details about these dietary options:

- **Grain-free** GF : Grain-free food is one of the fastest-growing segments of the commercial pet food world because more pet lovers are concerned about the high percentage of grains in traditional kibble. Can dogs eat grain? Certainly. But dogs have a tougher time digesting grains than humans do, partly because they lack the enzymes in their saliva to start digestion. Some dogs might even be allergic to grains (although dogs can definitely have allergies to beef, chicken, and other meats as well).

- **Paleo** P : As more people turn to a Paleo diet (which mimics the diet of the hunter-gatherer) for themselves, they also look to their dogs' diets and wonder what's biologically appropriate for their dog. Setting aside the convenience of the bag of kibble, what is most appropriate for dogs—animals that can eat as omnivores but whose teeth obviously say "carnivore"? Many people believe that a dog's ideal diet would be a canine version of the Paleo diet, most often referred to as an Ancestral Diet where dogs are concerned. This diet is higher in meat-based protein and fat and far lower in carbohydrates than commercial diets.

- **Raw** R : Perhaps no other canine diet is as hotly debated as the raw diet. Proponents point to the cleaner teeth, smaller stools, and excellent skin and coat of dogs on the raw diet. On the other side, detractors emphasize the risk (to both dogs and their humans) of bacteria spread when your dog eats raw meat, then kisses your toddler or chews on a toy that Grandma later picks up. Others point to the danger of eating whole bones (although not all raw feeders serve whole bones; some grind bones or add supplements).

If you do decide to switch to a specific specialty diet, make the transition gradually to avoid digestive problems that could arise from a sudden change in diet. (This gradual introduction is also recommended when switching from one commercial brand to another one.) Start by reducing the amount of "regular" food from your dog's diet, supplementing it with the specialty food, and then adjusting the relative amounts daily until you are feeding only the specialty diet. Typically 20–25 percent of your dog's diet should be switched out per day as you gradually change to the new diet.

One exception: If you're switching to a raw diet, you should know that most raw proponents recommend against a gradual transition from kibble to raw. Instead, most advise a twenty-four-hour fast before the switch; once that's done, they recommend a complete change to raw.

Our dogs have always been fed a varied diet. We give our dogs a wide range of foods all the time; their digestive systems have grown accustomed to a constant change of foods. Just as we eat a diverse diet, our dogs do as well. Unlike dogs who eat a diet of a single variety of kibble for months (or years) on end, our dogs are accustomed to one meal at breakfast and a totally different meal at dinner, and do well with the diversity. Every dog is an individual, however, so work with your veterinarian to determine what will work best for your dog.

SAVE MONEY

Making your own dog food can also save you money. Compared to the price of premium dog food (including commercial raw diets), homemade food can be a cost saver, especially when you consider that many of the ingredients are simple, staple items that you can purchase in bulk and store for future use. By using produce that is in season, you have the double advantage of having fresh ingredients at their nutritional peak available at the very lowest price.

Here's a quick look at some of the best seasonal buys:

- Fall: acorn squash, apples, butternut squash, figs, pears, pumpkin, sweet potatoes
- Winter: radishes, rutabagas, turnips
- Spring: apricots, carrots, mangos, spinach, strawberries, snow peas, sugar snap peas
- Summer: blackberries, blueberries, green beans, peaches, plums, raspberries, watermelon, zucchini

However, along with the immediate savings of making your own foods, there are also hidden economic benefits. By ensuring that your dogs have proper nutrition, you are giving them the foundation for excellent lifetime health, meaning far fewer visits to the veterinarian's office for expensive treatments and medications.

BEFORE YOU GIVE YOUR DOG A COMPLETELY HOMEMADE DIET . . .

Although it's easy to make your dog one or two homemade meals per week for variety, switching to a totally homemade diet isn't a change to be taken lightly. Dogs need

WHAT NOT TO FEED YOUR DOG

Before you begin spicing up Spot's supper, it's very important to realize that some foods that humans eat should never be fed to your dog. Among others, these are foods you must *not* feed your dog:

- **Alcohol**
- **Apple seeds**
- **Apricot pits**
- **Avocados**
- **Cherry pits**
- **Chocolate**
- **Coffee** (and other caffeinated drinks)
- **Garlic:** Some people feed small amounts but only in moderation. Ask your vet for recommendations.
- **Grapes and raisins:** Because they are condensed, raisins are more dangerous than grapes; avoid cereals and cookies with raisins.
- **Macadamia nuts**
- **Nutmeg**
- **Onions**
- **Peach pits**
- **Persimmon seeds**
- **Plum pits**
- **Potato peels** (green parts and eyes only; the rest of the skin is okay): Discard any green and sprouted portions of the potato. This includes all kinds of potatoes.
- **Tea**
- **Yeast dough:** Uncooked dough is very dangerous to your dog.
- **Xylitol:** A sweetener used in some diet foods and sugar-free gums, it is highly toxic to dogs.

balanced nutrition to help them live their best life, and figuring out that balance week in and week out can be daunting for some pet parents. After trying some of these recipes out on your dog, you may decide that you want to make your dog's principal diet homemade. Your first step is to schedule a talk with your veterinarian. Discuss the switch and get your vet's recommendations on foods and supplements for your dog's size, age, activity level, and any health concerns.

Your dog's life stage plays an important role in the formulation of a proper diet. Compared to adult dogs, puppies need a higher fat, protein, and calorie content in their food. Large and small dogs have varying needs as well; large breed pups need less calcium than their smaller cousins.

Did you know that too much of most nutritional elements can be just as harmful as too little? Yes, even too much of a good thing can lead to health problems. Here's some food for thought:

- Too much protein can overwork your dog's kidneys and liver as they work to remove the excess protein the body cannot absorb. (Too little protein can lead to growth problems for puppies.)

- Too much fat in your dog's diet can lead to, you guessed it, excess poundage on your pup! Too little fat, though, results in a dull coat and flaky skin.

- Too many vitamins can stress your dog's organs and even lead to bladder stones, while a lack of vitamins will make your tail-wagging chum tired and weak.

- Fiber also plays an important role in a balanced diet. Too much fiber leads to gas. Too little? Loose stools. Fiber is one component of your pet's diet that's easy to see (and suffer from) a lack of balance.

As you can see, obtaining the right balance involves many factors—but there are big benefits. Along with being in control of the ingredients that compose your dog's diet, you can also vary the diet according to your pooch's personal palate. Work closely with your dog's veterinarian to be sure your dog is getting everything he needs.

CHAPTER 2

The Ins and Outs of Cooking for Your Dog

We love cooking for our dogs. Why? Maybe it's the opportunity to really know what's in their food and to select healthy ingredients. Maybe it's the cost savings over premium treats. Or maybe it's just the boundless enthusiasm with which they greet our cooking.

Dogs don't worry about presentation. They don't concern themselves about the look of the plate it's served on. Dogs just want to enjoy the food you're giving them. They relish it with an enthusiasm that tells you that you *are* the next Julia Child.

But we'll be honest: It does take time to cook for your dogs. If you're considering a homemade diet, be sure to consider your schedule. Especially if you have large dogs (like we do), the time spent cooking the amount of food you need for a homemade diet is substantial. There are ways to streamline that cooking process, including cooking in bulk. Here are some tips for making the process as easy as possible.

SHOPPING FOR INGREDIENTS

Cooking your own dog treats and/or meals *can* be a money-saver—as long as you think ahead and shop with a plan. Here are some tips for buying ingredients inexpensively:

- **Look for "last chance" meats, fruits, and vegetables.** Although they're still safe to eat, these foods that are close to their expiration dates are often deeply discounted at grocery stores for a fast sale. In the case of fruits and vegetables, their ripe or slightly overripe state may make them less palatable to humans, but they'll be more easily digested by your dog.

🦴 **Check local farmers' markets for bruised or slightly damaged fruits and vegetables.** (Many markets welcome well-behaved dog shoppers as well!) Locally grown produce isn't just an eco-friendly choice, but a great way to save money and get foods at the peak of freshness. Buying bruised produce can be a great way to save on dog meal ingredients; many farmers will even give them away, especially if you're making another purchase.

🦴 **Buy less desirable cuts of meat.** Organ meats are inexpensive and make an important component of your dog's diet. If you are feeding a homemade diet, up to 10 percent of your dog's meal should include organ meats: liver, kidney, gizzards, and tripe. (Of that 10 percent, no more than half should be liver.) While these may not be at the top of the list for human shoppers, they're very popular with dogs—and they're an important nutritional source:

- **Liver:** Liver is a great source of vitamins A and B as well as iron. While it's a wonderful food (and a real favorite with most dogs), limit liver to just 5 percent of your dog's total diet so that your dog doesn't get too much vitamin A.
- **Heart:** Heart is actually considered a muscle meat, not an organ, so you can add more heart to your dog's meal without worry—which is a great thing because it's one of the most reasonably priced meats and one of the most nutritious. Beef heart contains thiamin, folate, selenium, phosphorus, zinc, CoQ10, vitamin B, amino acids, and more.
- **Tripe:** Cow stomach lining (although tripe can also refer to sheep, pig, goat, and deer stomachs) is sold in commercial grocery stores—but it has been washed and bleached and isn't nutritional. (You'll see that the tripe in the grocery store is sparkling white; it's used to make menudo.) Green tripe, rich with nutrients from the cow's diet, is made from the lining of the cow's fourth stomach, the abomasum. Green tripe isn't sold by butchers. Many pet parents feeding a raw diet will purchase frozen or dehydrated green tripe from commercial vendors.

BUYING MEAT IN BULK

If you decide to commit to a homemade diet—especially if you have large dogs—buying in bulk is a great way to save money. Meat is the ingredient that makes the most sense to buy in bulk—it can be expensive, and freezing it requires very little prep work. Regardless of whether you're preparing a cooked or a raw diet for your dog, buying meat in bulk can simplify meal preparation and save money at the same time. Consider these ideas:

- Share a bulk purchase. Often, homemade feeders who live near each other band together to purchase a side of beef or other large cut as a group.

- Ask other homemade feeders in your area to point you to good local meat sources: meat processing plants, wild game processors, and local butchers.

- Visit ethnic markets, which can be an excellent source for many organ meats and less-common cuts that aren't usually available at large grocery chains.

EQUIPMENT YOU NEED

Although your home kitchen has everything you need to prepare your dog's meals or treats, if you decide to get serious about a homemade diet, a few things can make the process much simpler:

- **Electric food grinder:** A food grinder is a very handy way to prepare an appropriate mix of meat and vegetables. Grinding your own meat is much less expensive than buying ground meat, and you can cut away the fat to prepare a healthier meal. Although less expensive grinders are available for $30–130, only heavy-duty commercial grinders in the $300–400 range are capable of grinding bones. Even with the more expensive models, grinding bones may void the warranty, so check with the manufacturer before purchase. Without bone in the meal, you'll need to supplement your dog's food. (More on supplements in

Chapter 3.)

🦴 **Food dehydrator:** Buying dehydrated meats and vegetables is convenient, but it's expensive! Make your own dehydrated jerky and chews on the cheap with a food dehydrator at a fraction of the cost. A food dehydrator is also excellent for drying vegetables and fruits during the peak season for use in later meals. Prices start at about $35 for basic dehydrators, although models with more controls can range from $200–300.

🦴 **Food scale:** To ensure that you are feeding your dog the proper amount of food every day, it's important to measure his food, both in terms of cups and weight. A digital kitchen food scale ranges from $10–50.

🦴 **Freezer:** Small chest freezers that provide storage for bulk meals for your dog start at about $200, ranging up to $1,000 for top-of-the-line models.

A Primer on Dog Nutrition

Dogs share many of the same nutritional needs as humans, requiring many of the same vitamins, minerals, proteins, and fats, although in different quantities. Like an infant, whose diet you completely control, your dog looks to you for all his nutritional needs. (We won't talk about the grass he scarfed down on your walk . . . or the lizard he caught in the backyard.) In general, you are responsible for the six nutrient groups your dog requires: vitamins, fat, minerals, carbohydrates, protein, and water.

HOW MUCH SHOULD MY DOG EAT?

As with humans, obesity is an epidemic in the dog world. The reason? Most people feed their dogs too much food. Feeding guidelines on bags of commercial food are just that: guidelines. They're written for unneutered adult dogs; spayed and neutered dogs have lower metabolic rates and need slightly less food. Also, many pet parents don't measure their dog's portions, instead filling the plate or (worse) "free feeding" with a bowl full of food that the dog is allowed to eat at will throughout the day.

Instead, it's best to measure your dog's food for twice-daily feedings. (Feed puppies three to four times per day.) The rule of thumb is that your dog should eat about 2.5 percent of his weight per day. You'll adjust this up or down depending on your dog's activity level and if you're trying to maintain his weight, trim a little off, or put on some weight. For a 100-pound dog, that translates into about 2.5 pounds of food per day, or 1.25 pounds of food per meal.

FEEDING GUIDELINES BY BREED AND WEIGHT

Breed/Average Weight	Daily Serving
Chihuahua/6 pounds	.15 pound per day
Shetland Sheepdog/20 pounds	.5 pound per day
Dachshund/20–25 pounds	.5–.625 pound per day
Beagle/25 pounds	.625 pound per day
Poodle/45–70 pounds	1.125–1.75 pounds per day
Bulldog/50 pounds	1.25 pounds per day
Golden Retriever/60–80 pounds	1.5–2 pounds per day
Labrador Retriever/75 pounds	1.875 pounds per day
German Shepherd/75–95 pounds	1.875–2.25 pounds per day
Greyhound/80 pounds	2 pounds per day
Rottweiler/90–110 pounds	2.25–2.75 pounds per day
Great Dane/120 pounds	3 pounds per day

This is, of course, a very broad guide, one that varies with the food you're feeding, your dog's activity level, your dog's age, and any relevant medical conditions. (If your dog will be outdoors hiking around with you during cold weather, he'll need more food. If your dog is pregnant, she'll need more food.) This table gives you a general baseline to start from, though, and you can work from there, as you see if your dog is still hungry after the meal or if your dog is gaining/losing weight.

A NOTE ABOUT SERVING SIZES

You'll see that the recipes in this book often yield much more than a dog would eat at a single sitting. Use this table to determine how much food your dog needs in a day, then plan appropriate serving sizes for his meals and treats accordingly. Use the storage information given to safely store and/or freeze remaining prepared food.

Although indulgent dog guardians may sometime fail to notice that their pooch is packing extra pounds, it's easy to ask your veterinarian if your dog might be overweight. You can then monitor your dog's weight with a periodic hands-on examination by feeling his ribs. If you are able to feel his ribs, he is usually not overweight. Your dog's ribs should feel much like the back of your hand. Also, look at your dog from above and see if his waist is visible: It should show tapering from behind his rib cage toward his tail. From the side, you should also be able to discern an upward "tummy tuck" in his abdomen area.

SETTING UP A FEEDING SCHEDULE

Whether you are feeding a homemade or a commercial diet or a combination of the two, it is also important to establish a feeding schedule for your dog. Your objective is to make sure your dogs receive proper nutrition without becoming overweight. Just as with humans, dogs that are overweight become susceptible to various health issues, including extra stress on their joints, lethargy, liver disease, and diabetes.

Although an adult dog may be able to receive adequate nutrition from one large meal daily, breaking it up into two smaller meals served twice a day may reduce the chance of bloat, especially if your canine wolfs down his food. Plus, it gives you twice as many chances to bond with your dog via your homemade food! You can also use mealtime as a quick training exercise, asking your dog to sit and wait politely for your "okay" signal before diving in to enjoy the meal.

A DOG'S COMPLETE AND BALANCED DIET

If you look at most commercial dog foods, you'll see the phrase "complete and balanced" splashed on the packaging somewhere. This means that the food has been formulated to include the key nutrients in your dog's diet in balanced proportions: vitamins, fat, minerals, carbohydrates, protein, and water. A complete and balanced commercial dog food means that it is complete as it is, with no supplements required.

It's important that dogs be fed a complete and balanced diet—but that doesn't mean that each and every meal be completely balanced, as it is with commercial foods. Our own human diets balance out over time. Through the week, we all eat a wide variety of foods that give us nutrition in different forms. Together, they come together to provide a complete and balanced diet. We normally don't eat one particular meal that answers all our nutritional needs. The same can be done with our dogs. Your dog's diet can be diversified from meal to meal, balancing out over the breakfasts and dinners served throughout the week.

Calcium

However, you will generally need to add a supplement to your dog's diet—if not a general multivitamin, then at least a calcium supplement because dogs have a much higher need for calcium than humans. Unless you feed your dog raw bones or include nutritional-grade bone meal in their food, you'll need to offer a calcium supplement. (It's also very important to have the correct calcium-to-phosphorus ratio. Talk with your veterinarian about a range for your dog; in general, the ideal range of calcium to phosphorus is about 1.5 to 1.)

In this book, you'll find a recipe for making your own eggshell calcium, which many pet parents prefer over bone meal because bones can store impurities (and because bone meal is often made from bones that have been used to make gelatin, so many nutrients are already missing from the bones). As with most things related to dog nutrition, the recommended amount of calcium varies, but expect to supplement with about one 600 mg calcium supplement per 10 to 15 pounds of adult dog. If you're mixing homemade and commercial food, only add supplements for the portion of homemade diet, not the total.

Other Vitamins and Minerals

It's no secret that manufacturers of commercial dog food usually add nutritional additives to their formulas, in part to replace nutrients that are lost during processing and production of the foods. The processing of dry commercial dog food often includes a high heat extrusion process that can destroy natural nutrients. The result is food that then must be refortified with supplemental additives to meet dogs' nutritional requirements. Making your dog homemade dishes can be a healthy alternative to feeding commercial products because you're offering meals that retain natural nutrients such as vitamins, minerals, protein, fiber, and fatty acids.

When considering what to cook for your dog, it is tempting to think in terms of human food consumption and human nutrition. "If it fulfills *my* nutritional needs, it must also fulfill my dog's" is reasoning that, though understandable, is seriously flawed because the canine's digestive system is not the same as that of a human. Many of the same nutritional building blocks are there, but they must be offered in different ratios and quantities.

The vitamin building blocks of your dog's diet include:

- **Vitamin A:** Found in liver and fish oil, vitamin A boosts the immune system and aids skin and ocular health.

- **Vitamin C:** This also boosts the immune system and promotes healthy cells. Vitamin C is found in many vegetable oils.

- **Vitamin D:** Liver is a great source of vitamin D, which strengthens bones and teeth.

- **Vitamin E:** Found in vegetable oils, this vitamin boosts the immune system and encourages healthy cell production.

Minerals are also essential for a balanced diet and include:

- **Calcium:** Calcium is essential for bones and teeth as well as for muscle function and blood clotting. It's found in bone, blood, eggshells, and nutritional-grade bone meal.

- **Phosphorus:** This mineral nurtures bones and teeth as well as healthy cells and muscles. As noted above, it's important to have the correct calcium-to-phosphorus ratio. This mineral is found in meats as well as in dairy products and eggs.

- **Sodium:** This nutrient promotes healthy muscles and helps maintain your dog's fluid levels.

Essential fatty acids are also important in a complete diet:

- **Omega-6** is vital for coat care, giving your dog rich, lustrous fur. Sunflower or safflower oil added to your dog's diet (about 1 teaspoon for a small dog or 1 tablespoon for a large dog) can keep your dog's coat shiny.

- **Omega-3** fatty acids benefit your dog's skin and can be found in flaxseed oil or fish oil (including sardines, one of our dogs' favorites).

TREATING YOUR DOG

Whether you use them for training purposes or just to reward your dog for being your buddy, making your own treats gives you control over his nutritional components as well as his size.

How Many Treats Should You Give?

Of course, giving extra treats between meals has the potential for busting your dog's diet. Some willpower is in order, both for you and your dog! Treats should never make up more than 10 percent of your dog's total diet.

Training with Treats

We love using training treats with our dogs; both our dogs have learned very quickly thanks to positive reinforcement training. Remember that you'll need many training treats when initially training your dog, so the key is to make training treats very small (think pea-size) and then compensate by reducing your dog's meal size.

Meat treats work best with many dogs, and often the stronger-scented treats like liver are most effective. Allowing refrigerated treats to warm to room temperature before you use them will bring out the scent to further entice your dog. You'll also get the best results if the training treats are used exclusively for training.

Many trainers also use a dog's regular meal as a training tool, meaning that you can give out far more "treats" as positive reinforcement training tools. A serving of chicken, which might have comprised your dog's dinner, can be cut into small bits and used as training treats instead.

Bones: Yes or No?

Should you give your dog bones as a chew toy? That's definitely a bone of contention in the dog world! First, the easy answer: you should never give your dog cooked bones. The cooking process dehydrates the bones, making them far more likely to splinter and break. Splintered bones can puncture an organ and lead to life-threatening complications.

Beyond that, though, things get a little stickier. Ask most raw-food diet advocates, and you'll hear that raw bones—from large marrow bones to smaller chicken wings and thighs—play an important role in their dog's diet. Digestible bones (comprising up to 10 percent of the diet) provide the necessary calcium your dog requires, and large marrow bones are a recreational favorite and are also an excellent source of vitamins and minerals.

On the flip side, even raw bones present a danger. The American Veterinary Medical Association (AVMA) says, "Bones or bone fragments in some raw diets can result in intestinal obstruction or perforation, gastroenteritis, and fractured teeth." We can testify to the fractured teeth: Our Irie, a devoted marrow bone chewer, had to have three teeth extracted due to fractured teeth.

The decision to feed bones, whether as part of a diet or as an occasional treat, is one that you will need to make after consulting with your veterinarian.

CHAPTER 4

Sweet Treats

Does your dog have a sweet tooth? Although you should never feed a dog chocolate, which is toxic to canines, many other sweets are fine for rewarding your rover. Blackstrap molasses, which is rich in nutrients, serves as a sweetener for many of these recipes, while others rely on fruits for their touch of sweetness. You'll be able to take advantage of seasonal sales as well as peak harvest seasons for preparing wholesome treats with a hint of pear, pumpkin, blueberries, and more.

Grain-Free Peanut Butter Biscuits GF

Most dogs, ours included, absolutely love peanut butter. This easy recipe is grain-free; if your dog has no issues with wheat, you can substitute whole-wheat flour or all-purpose flour for chickpea flour.

YIELDS: 36 (2") treats

1 medium banana, mashed

3 tablespoons organic unsweetened creamy peanut butter

1 egg

1¾ cups chickpea flour

1. Preheat oven to 350°F. Grease a cookie sheet or line with parchment paper.

2. In a large bowl, mix banana, peanut butter, egg, and flour. Turn out dough on a floured surface and knead; roll out the dough to ¼" thickness.

3. Cut dough into 24 cookies with cookie cutters (or slice with a pizza cutter) and place on cookie sheet. Bake for 25 minutes or until golden brown.

4. Cool completely before serving or refrigerating. Refrigerate for 5 days or freeze in an airtight container for up to 6 months.

Flour Power

Chickpeas, also known as garbanzo beans, are a good source of fiber and protein as well as minerals including manganese and copper. They are also low in cholesterol, sodium, and saturated fats. Flour ground from the beans makes a good alternative to traditional grain flours. You'll find it at health food stores, farmers' markets, and at grocery stores that specialize in Middle Eastern foods.

Coconut Carrot Treats GF P

This Paleo treat is also grain-free, thanks to the coconut flour. Along with being tasty to dogs, coconut is rich in potassium and many other vitamins and minerals.

YIELDS: 36 (2") treats

½ pound carrots, cut into 1" rounds

¼ cup coconut chips

2 eggs

¼ cup coconut flour

1. Preheat oven to 350°F. Grease a cookie sheet or line with parchment paper.

2. Place carrots in a blender along with coconut chips, blending to a fine chop.

3. In a medium bowl, add carrot–coconut chip mixture, eggs, and flour. Stir until mixed completely.

4. Use a spoon or melon baller to scoop out 1 tablespoon dough; drop onto cookie sheet. Flatten lightly with a fork. Repeat until all batter is used.

5. Bake cookies for 40 minutes or until golden brown.

6. Cool completely before serving or refrigerating. Refrigerate for 5 days or freeze in an airtight container for up to 6 months.

·············· **Coconut Is Brain Food** ···············

Studies have shown coconut oil to be beneficial in improving brain function, including in dogs with canine cognitive dysfunction. Look for unrefined, cold-pressed coconut oil to add to your dog's diet.

Paleo Pooch Treats GF P

Your dog doesn't have to be on the Paleo diet to enjoy this tasty treat. It's also grain-free!

YIELDS: 36 (2") treats

2 tablespoons water

1½ tablespoons ground flaxseed

1 sweet potato, peeled, boiled, and mashed

1 egg

¼ cup coconut milk

½ cup organic unsweetened peanut butter

½ cup coconut flour

1. Preheat oven to 350°F. Grease a cookie sheet or line with parchment paper.

2. In a small bowl, add water to the flaxseed to form a paste as you work on other ingredients.

3. In a large bowl, combine sweet potato, egg, coconut milk, peanut butter, and coconut flour, mixing well.

4. Add flax paste and continue to mix.

5. Use a spoon or melon baller to scoop out 1 tablespoon of dough; drop dough onto cookie sheet. Flatten lightly with a fork. Repeat until all batter is used.

6. Bake for 40–45 minutes until golden brown.

7. Remove from heat and cool on a wire rack before serving or refrigerating. Refrigerate for 5 days or freeze in an airtight container for up to 6 months.

Peanut Butter Chia Treats

Combine the powerful nutritional punch of chia seeds with the yummy goodness of peanut butter for a treat that's filled with antioxidants, calcium, and omega-3 fatty acids.

YIELDS: 36 (2") treats

1½ cups rolled oats

1 teaspoon baking powder

2 tablespoons chia seeds

½ cup all-purpose or wheat flour

¾ cup organic unsweetened peanut butter

2 eggs

1 tablespoon blackstrap molasses

¼ cup coconut oil

1. Preheat oven to 350°F. Grease a cookie sheet or line with parchment paper.

2. In a medium bowl, whisk oats, baking powder, chia seeds, and flour. Set aside.

3. Use a mixer to combine peanut butter, eggs, molasses, and coconut oil. Gradually add dry mix to the wet mixture, and continue to mix until combined. Use a spoon or melon baller to scoop out 1 tablespoon dough; drop onto cookie sheet. Repeat until all batter is used.

4. Bake for 10–15 minutes until golden brown.

5. Cool completely before serving or refrigerating. Refrigerate for 5 days or freeze in an airtight container for up to 6 months.

Blueberry Fruit Rollups GF P

Blueberries form the base for this snack to share with Spot—but feel free to substitute other fruits in season. The rollups make a great treat for long dog walks and can easily be torn into small pieces.

YIELDS: 5 (1½" × 6") strips

1 pound fresh or frozen blueberries

1 tablespoon lemon juice

1 tablespoon raw honey

1. Preheat oven to 170°F. Line a cookie sheet with parchment paper.

2. Place all ingredients in a blender and purée. Add a tablespoon of water if necessary.

3. Spread mixture over parchment paper, avoiding the edges of the paper.

4. Bake 6–7 hours until the rollups are no longer sticky. Remove from oven and cool completely.

5. Cut into strips and refrigerate. Refrigerate for 5 days.

Berry, Berry Good Rollups

These treats are easy to make in a dehydrator as well! Cut parchment paper to fit your dehydrator trays, being careful to leave plenty of room for air flow. Rearrange the trays every few hours for even drying; remove from dehydrator when no longer sticky.

Growling Granola Bars

Traditional granola bars have too much sugar for dogs. These easy bars get their sweetness from healthy peanut butter and molasses.

YIELDS: 36 (1") squares

3½ cups old-fashioned oats

½ teaspoon cinnamon

1 tablespoon blackstrap molasses

1 cup organic unsweetened peanut butter

¼ cup water

½ cup Pumpkin Purée (see Chapter 15)

¼ cup applesauce

¼ cup honey

¼ cup dry roasted peanuts, finely chopped

1. Preheat oven to 350°F. Use nonstick cooking spray to lightly grease an 8" x 8" pan.

2. Place all ingredients in a large bowl, stirring the heavy mixture until all oats are moist.

3. Press the mixture into the prepared pan and bake on the center rack for 30 minutes.

4. Remove from oven and cool on a wire rack. When cool, transfer to refrigerator for at least 4 hours to set.

5. Cut into squares. Refrigerate for 5 days or freeze in an airtight container for up to 6 months.

········· **Measure Molasses Carefully!** ·········

Blackstrap molasses is rich with potassium and minerals; many swear by it for alleviating their dog's symptoms of arthritis. However, avoid adding too much molasses to your dog's diet or it can cause digestive upset.

PB and Pumpkin Treats

You might try popping one of these yourself as you give your dog one! If it's not sweet enough for your consumption, just add some peanut butter icing. For this recipe, you can use either canned pumpkin purée (but *not* pumpkin pie filling, which has spices and too much sugar) or homemade Pumpkin Purée (see Chapter 15).

YIELDS: 30 (2") treats

2½ cups whole-wheat flour

½ cup pumpkin purée

½ cup organic unsweetened peanut butter

2 teaspoons cinnamon

1 teaspoon baking powder

½ cup water, as needed

1. Preheat oven to 350°F. Grease two cookie sheets or line with parchment paper.

2. In a medium bowl, mix all ingredients except the water, then add it sparingly (the amount of water needed will depend on the oil content in the peanut butter).

3. Turn out dough on a floured surface and knead; roll out the dough to ¼" thickness. Cut into 30 fun shapes. Place dough on prepared cookie sheets.

4. Bake for 20 minutes, then remove from oven and cool. Be sure to cool the treats completely before serving or refrigerating. Refrigerate for 5 days or freeze in an airtight container for up to 6 months.

Some Spices Nicer Than Others

Some studies have shown that cinnamon has both antioxidant and antibacterial qualities—plus it's just plain tasty to your dog. As tempting and flavorful as spices are, though, don't include nutmeg in your dog's treats. It can cause both a high heart rate and hallucinations in dogs.

Cranberry Dog Treats

Autumn's most popular berry lends a holiday feel to these treats. Cranberry has long been known for its role in preventing urinary tract infections; it's also rich in vitamin C, fiber, manganese, and antioxidants.

YIELDS: 40 (2") treats

1 cup cranberries

2 cups whole-wheat flour

2 cups all-purpose flour

1 cup oats

1 teaspoon cinnamon

1 teaspoon baking powder

4 tablespoons (¼ cup) butter, melted

1 egg

¼ cup molasses

½ cup water, as needed

1. Preheat oven to 350°F. Grease two cookie sheets or line with parchment paper.

2. Toss cranberries into a blender or food processor and chop. Mix flours, oats, cinnamon, and baking powder in a large bowl, then add the melted butter, chopped cranberries, egg, and molasses. Slowly add the water, a little bit at a time.

3. Mix the dough until just combined. Turn out dough on a lightly floured surface and knead; roll out the dough to ¼" thickness. Use cookie cutters to cut into 40 desired shapes.

4. Place the treats on the cookie sheets and bake for 30 minutes.

5. Cool completely before serving or refrigerating. Refrigerate for 5 days or freeze in an airtight container for up to 6 months.

Is Your Canine Craving Some Crunch?

Some dogs absolutely love the crunch of a treat (which also can help to clean their teeth). If you'd like to make your treats extra crunchy, at the end of baking, turn off the oven and allow the treats to cool in the oven for 3–4 hours. Slightly crack the oven door to allow any moisture to escape as the treats dry out and cool.

Elvis Peanut Butter and Banana Sandwich Dog Treats

To make this treat a little healthier for your hound dog, we have substituted the white bread Elvis loved for wheat bread in our list of ingredients.

YIELDS: 1 serving

2 tablespoons organic unsweetened peanut butter

2 slices wheat bread

1 ripe banana, mashed

2 tablespoons bacon grease, butter, or cooking oil

1. Spread the peanut butter on one slice of bread and the mashed banana on the other slice of bread. Place the halves together to assemble.

2. On low heat, heat the grease (or oil or butter) in a medium skillet. Grill the sandwich until it's golden brown, about 3 minutes on each side.

3. Let the sandwich cool, then cut into small pieces with a knife or cookie cutters. (Don't try to cut it while the sandwich is hot or the peanut butter will run out!)

4. Cool before refrigerating or serving that day to your dog. (This treat can be refrigerated, but the bread will lose its crispness.) Refrigerate for up to 5 days.

Fine-Tune the Grease Factor

Elvis loved his sandwich grilled using bacon grease, but you can substitute butter or another type of cooking oil. You can also make this on an electric nonstick grill without oil.

Pear and Molasses Dog Biscuits

Don't feed your dog pear seeds—or apple seeds, either—but the flesh of the pear makes a healthy treat. Pears are a good source of water-soluble fiber as well as vitamin C. Softer pear varieties like Bartlett are easier to digest than the crisper Asian varieties.

YIELDS: 16 (3") treats

2 cups pears, cored and chopped

2½ cups whole-wheat flour

¼ cup water

1 tablespoon baking powder

3 tablespoons molasses

1. Preheat oven to 350°F. Grease a cookie sheet or line with parchment paper.

2. Mix all ingredients in a large bowl. The result is a very sticky, heavy dough. Turn out dough on a lightly floured surface and knead; roll out the dough to about ¼" thickness. Cut dough into 16 squares.

3. Place the biscuits on cookie sheet.

4. Bake for 30 minutes (the bottom of the biscuits should be golden brown when done), then cool the biscuits completely before refrigerating or serving. Refrigerate for up to 5 days or freeze in an airtight container for up to 6 months.

Prized Pear Wood

Did you know that pear wood is often used for kitchen spoons and stirrers because it won't add any flavor or color to the food? It also stands up to repeated washing and drying in the kitchen.

Peanut Butter Bones

This recipe—which will fill your kitchen with the scent of fresh-baked cookies—is one of our dogs' favorites. If you want to decorate the treats with icing for a special event, purée the carrots for a smoother texture.

YIELDS: 24 (2") treats

1 cup whole-wheat flour

1 cup all-purpose flour

1 cup multigrain cereal or bran flakes, crushed

2 tablespoons baking powder

½ cup shredded carrots

2 tablespoons olive oil

1 tablespoon blackstrap molasses

1 cup organic unsweetened peanut butter (creamy or crunchy)

½ cup water

1. Preheat oven to 350°F. Grease a cookie sheet or line with parchment paper.

2. Mix dry ingredients in a large bowl, then add carrots, olive oil, molasses, and peanut butter, adding water a little at a time. The amount of water you'll need will vary based on the oil in the peanut butter.

3. Turn out dough on a lightly floured surface and knead; roll out the dough to ¼" thickness. Cut into 24 shapes with a cookie cutter.

4. Place the treats on the cookie sheet.

5. Bake for 30 minutes or until golden brown.

6. After baking the bones until browned on both sides, remove from the oven, set them out on a wire rack, and let them cool completely to make them crisper. Refrigerate for 5 days or freeze in an airtight container for up to 6 months.

No Raisins, Please!

Never include cereals with raisins in dog treat recipes. Raisins (and grapes) are toxic to most dogs and can result in acute renal failure. Raisin toxicity can develop within hours of ingesting.

Peanut Butter and Applesauce Dog Biscuits

This tasty recipe is especially fun to make when apples are in season. It's easy to make your own unsweetened applesauce; just wash, core, and peel the apples (remember, apple seeds are toxic to dogs). Dice the apples and place in a large pot with enough water to cover them and bring near boiling. Turn down the heat and cook until soft. Drain, then purée in a blender and refrigerate, or jar or freeze for future use.

YIELDS: 36 (2") treats

- 3 cups whole-wheat flour
- 2 cups oats
- 1 cup organic unsweetened peanut butter
- 1 cup unsweetened applesauce
- 1 teaspoon baking powder

1. Preheat oven to 350°F. Grease two cookie sheets or line with parchment paper.

2. Mix all ingredients in a large bowl, stirring until well mixed and ready for kneading. Knead the dough on a lightly floured surface. Depending on the oil in your peanut butter, you might have to add a teaspoon of olive oil if you find the mixture is a little too crumbly.

3. Roll the dough out to about ¼" thickness, then cut the dough into 36 desired shapes. Place on your cookie sheets.

4. Bake for 25 minutes until lightly browned. Remove from the oven and cool completely before serving or refrigerating. Refrigerate for 5 days or freeze in an airtight container for up to 6 months.

Pumpkin Mini Muffins

If you don't have homemade Pumpkin Purée (see Chapter 15), use half a can of puréed pumpkin (not pumpkin pie filling) for this easy recipe.

YIELDS: 36 mini muffins

1⅔ cups rice flour

1 teaspoon baking soda

½ teaspoon cinnamon

2 tablespoons molasses

1¾ cups pumpkin purée

½ cup canola oil

2 eggs, lightly beaten

⅓ cup water

1. Preheat oven to 350°F. Spray three mini-muffin tins or line with parchment cups.

2. In a large bowl, mix rice flour, baking soda, cinnamon, and molasses, then add pumpkin purée, oil, and eggs. As needed, add water until the mixture is the consistency of mashed potatoes.

3. Drop spoonfuls of mixture into muffin cups, filling ⅔ of the way.

4. Bake for 20 minutes or until a toothpick inserted in the center of a muffin comes out clean.

5. Cool completely before serving or refrigerating. Refrigerate for 5 days or freeze in an airtight container for up to 6 months.

Keep Treats the Same Size

Even if you use fun cookie cutter shapes, be sure to keep the biscuits fairly uniform in size so they will bake and brown evenly in the oven. Another tip to keep in mind is to roll the dough thinner for a crisp consistency, and thicker for chewier biscuits. (A thinner dough will yield more treats than the yield shows.)

Banana Sunflower Dog Cookies

These sunny cookies are sure to brighten Fido's day.

YIELDS: 24 (2") cookies

3 bananas, mashed

½ cup canola oil

2–2½ cups all-purpose flour

1 cup shelled, unsalted sunflower seeds

1 tablespoon baking powder

1 teaspoon baking soda

1. In a large bowl, mix all ingredients until well blended. (Add more flour if the mixture is too wet—it will depend on the size of the bananas.) Refrigerate bowl for at least 30 minutes.

2. Preheat oven to 350°F. Grease a cookie sheet or line with parchment paper.

3. Roll dough into 24 small balls. Place on cookie sheet, then flatten with a fork. Bake for 10–20 minutes until golden brown.

4. Remove from oven and cool completely before serving or refrigerating. Refrigerate for 5 days or freeze in an airtight container for up to 6 months.

Not Just for the Birds

Packed with vitamin E, the little sunflower seed is a treasure chest of goodness for your dog. Skin and coat benefits are some of the best reasons to feed these seeds to your dog, but they also have anti-inflammatory, anti-cancer, and heart-health benefits! You can also feed raw sunflower seeds to your dog, but always shell the seeds first.

Banana Vegan Cupcakes

These easy-to-make vegan cupcakes come together in just minutes and make a tasty snack to share with your dog!

YIELDS: 24 mini cupcakes

2 ripe bananas, mashed

2 tablespoons agave nectar

⅓ cup unsweetened applesauce

3 cups whole-wheat flour

1½–2 teaspoons organic baking powder

2 cups water

1. Preheat oven to 350°F. Spray mini-cupcake tins or line with parchment cups.

2. In a large bowl, mix bananas, agave nectar, and applesauce; slowly add in flour and baking powder, adding water a bit at a time.

3. Pour mix into cupcake tins, filling ⅔ of the way. Bake for 15 minutes or until a toothpick inserted in the center of a cupcake comes out clean.

4. Cool completely before serving or refrigerating. Refrigerate for 5 days or freeze in an airtight container for up to 6 months.

Good Breath Dog Treats

Parsley is a natural breath freshener for your dog to help avoid doggie breath! Some dogs have an aversion to having their teeth brushed, so parsley-based foods can really help between brushings and dental cleanings, which are an important part of your dog's overall health.

YIELDS: 24 (2") treats

2 cups whole-wheat flour

1 cup rolled oats

½ cup nonfat dry milk powder

2 tablespoons chopped fresh parsley

2 large eggs

1 cup organic unsweetened peanut butter

½ cup water

1. Preheat oven to 300°F. Grease a cookie sheet or line with parchment paper.

2. Whisk together flour, oats, nonfat dry milk powder, and parsley in a large bowl. Set aside. In another bowl, beat eggs, then add peanut butter and water. Mix well, then slowly add wet ingredients to dry.

3. Turn out dough on a floured surface and knead; roll out the dough to ¼" thickness.

4. Cut into 24 shapes with cookie cutters and bake for 30 minutes or until golden.

5. Cool completely before serving or refrigerating. Refrigerate for 5 days or freeze in an airtight container for up to 6 months.

A Breath of Fresh Air

Be sure that "doggie breath" isn't a sign of an underlying problem, like an abscessed tooth or gingivitis. Your veterinarian can tell you if your dog just needs a breath cleanser or a dental cleaning.

Pumpkin Gingersnaps

Fresh ginger adds a delightfully fragrant touch to these treats. If you don't have fresh ginger, you can substitute ground ginger, although it isn't as flavorful.

YIELDS: 36 (2") cookies

2½ cups all-purpose flour

1½ teaspoons baking soda

4 tablespoons (¼ cup) butter, warmed to room temperature

1 egg, at room temperature

4 teaspoons peeled and finely grated fresh ginger

½ cup Pumpkin Purée (see Chapter 15)

1. Preheat oven to 350°F. Grease a cookie sheet or line with parchment paper.

2. In a medium bowl, combine flour and baking soda, then add butter, egg, ginger, and pumpkin. Mix thoroughly.

3. Turn out dough on a floured surface and knead until completely combined. Roll out dough to ¼" thickness and cut into 36 shapes with cookie cutters. (If you'd like a chewier treat, you can roll dough to ½" thickness.)

4. Place cookies on cookie sheet; bake for 15 minutes on the middle rack of the oven.

5. Remove cookies from oven and cool completely on a wire rack before serving or refrigerating. Refrigerate for 5 days or freeze in an airtight container for up to 6 months.

Easy Pumpkin Drops

This super-simple recipe isn't just easy on you—it's also an excellent choice for senior dogs or for dogs with wheat allergies. Pumpkin is a great ingredient for all dogs; its rich orange color hints at the lutein, alpha carotene, and beta carotene contained inside. If your dog doesn't have any wheat allergies, feel free to substitute Cream of Wheat in this recipe.

YIELDS: 24 (2") treats

2 cups Pumpkin Purée
(see Chapter 15)

¾ cup Cream of Rice cereal

½ cup nonfat dry milk powder

1. Preheat oven to 300°F. Grease a cookie sheet or line with parchment paper.

2. In a large bowl, mix all ingredients.

3. Drop dough onto cookie sheet, 1 tablespoon at a time. Flatten slightly if you like, or leave as small balls.

4. Bake for 20 minutes or until golden brown.

5. Cool completely before serving or refrigerating. Refrigerate for 5 days or freeze in an airtight container for up to 6 months.

Ancient Goodness

Did you know that the oldest evidence of pumpkin (found in Mexico) dates back to 7000–5500 B.C.? This North American native pumpkin now yields 1.5 billion pounds of crop every year. The world record pumpkin weighed nearly 500 pounds. Snoopy and Linus would agree that's definitely a Great Pumpkin!

CHAPTER 5

Savory Treats

Not every dog has a sweet tooth; some are far more motivated by savory treats. Our Tiki loves meaty treats (the stronger scented, the better). If your dog likes savory treats, you can also use small portions of meals as treats, whether given singly or served inside a stuffable toy like a KONG®. Liver is the base of savory treats favored by many dogs. You can use beef or chicken livers—organic is always best for a "filtering" organ such as liver. Because of the high level of vitamin A, liver of any kind should be served in small doses, never more than 5 percent of your dog's daily diet.

Cheese Crisps GF

If your dog doesn't have any trouble digesting lactose, these easy cheese bites make a powerful training treat (and you'll find they're as addictive as potato chips for the trainer, too!).

YIELDS: 16 (2") treats

- 1 cup grated hard cheese such as Asiago, Parmesan (not powdered), or Romano
- 1 teaspoon garlic powder (optional)

1. Preheat oven to 350°F. Line two cookie sheets with parchment paper.

2. If you are using garlic powder, toss with the cheese. Don't mash the ingredients together—simply pile or stack about 1 tablespoon of cheese onto parchment, allowing at least 2" between treats because they will spread out. If any pieces of cheese are standing up too tall, even out the pile, so each treat is roughly the same height.

3. Bake for about 5 minutes.

4. Cool before serving. Refrigerate for 5 days.

People-Friendly Dog Food

These Cheese Crisps are especially great for people; try serving with dips as a substitute for tortilla or potato chips.

Raw Carrot Pops GF R

Make these pops tiny to use as training treats, or to plug into a stuffable treat-dispensing toy!

YIELDS: 36 (2") treats

4 ounces reduced-fat cream cheese

1 cup finely grated carrots

½ cup unsalted peanuts

1. In a medium bowl, combine cream cheese and carrots.

2. Using a blender or food processor, chop peanuts to a fine powder. Pour out powder onto a clean surface.

3. With a spoon or melon baller, roll small bits of cream cheese mixture into a small ball, approximately 1" in diameter. Roll in peanut powder and place on a cookie sheet.

4. Treats can be stored in the refrigerator for 5 days. For longer storage, place treats on a cookie sheet and freeze for 4 hours. Once frozen, bag treats in an airtight container; they'll keep for up to 6 months. You can serve them frozen or thawed.

Liver Cupcakes GF P

Liver may not make *your* mouth water, but your dog feels differently! We use pieces of the popular cupcakes as powerful training treats.

YIELDS: 36 mini cupcakes

1 pound chicken liver, rinsed

3 eggs

4 tablespoons (¼ cup) butter

2 cups Pumpkin Purée (see Chapter 15)

3 cups coconut flour

1 teaspoon baking powder

1. Preheat oven to 350°F. Spray mini-cupcake tins or line with cupcake cups.

2. Purée chicken liver in a blender.

3. Once puréed, add eggs, butter, and pumpkin. Pulse to combine in blender. In a large bowl, mix purée with flour and baking powder.

4. Fill muffin tins ⅔ of the way, and bake for 25 minutes.

5. Remove from heat and cool completely before serving or refrigerating. Refrigerate for 3 days or freeze in an airtight container for up to 6 months.

Tuna Crackers

**We all like a little crunch now and then! These tasty crackers
(which also make nice little appetizers for you) are easy to make and
flavorful as training treat bits, too. With its high mercury content
(higher in white albacore than chunked light or white tuna),
tuna should be only an occasional treat for your dog.**

YIELDS: 40 (1") crackers

1 (5-ounce) can chunked light or white tuna packed in water, undrained

1 cup cornmeal

1 cup all-purpose flour

⅓ cup water

1. Preheat oven to 350°F. Grease a cookie sheet or line with parchment paper.

2. Mix all ingredients by hand. Turn out dough on a floured surface and knead; roll out the dough to ¼" thickness.

3. Place dough on cookie sheet; cut with a pizza cutter into 40 crackers. Bake for 20 minutes until golden.

4. Turn off oven, and allow treats to continue cooling in oven. Cool completely before serving.

5. Refrigerate for 3 days or freeze in an airtight container for up to 6 months.

Just a Hint of Tuna

Along with using tuna meat in dog recipes, you can also substitute tuna juice in place of water in treat recipes for an extra taste boost.

Chicken Liver and Green Bean Biscuits

Although liver should only make up 5 percent of your dog's diet, it makes a flavorful addition to dog treats. This quick recipe calls for canned green beans, but you can cook a half-pound of fresh green beans instead!

YIELDS: 35–40 (2") biscuits

1 pound chicken liver, rinsed

1 (14.5-ounce) can green beans, no salt added, drained

5 cups whole-wheat flour

2 cups brown rice flour

1 egg

1. Preheat oven to 350°F. Grease two cookie sheets or line with parchment paper.

2. In a food processor or blender, purée chicken livers, then add green beans. Pulse until puréed with only small chunks remaining.

3. In a large bowl, mix flours and egg, then pour in chicken liver and green bean mixture. Mix dough (by hand or with a dough hook). The dough will be heavy.

4. Roll dough to ½" thickness, then cut with your favorite cookie cutters. (Alternatively, pinch off a small piece of dough, roll it into a ball, place on cookie sheet, and slightly flatten with a fork.)

5. Bake treats for 30 minutes; watch for treats to brown on the bottom.

6. Remove from oven and cool on a wire rack before refrigerating or serving. Refrigerate for 3 days or freeze in an airtight container for up to 6 months.

·············· **Finish with a Flourish** ··············

To create a little glaze on these treats, whip an egg, then dip the top of the biscuits in the egg mixture. Return the biscuits to the oven for another 2 minutes.

Deli Turkey Rollups GF

Low-sodium turkey forms the base for this easy appetizer for you and your dog to share! They only take minutes to prepare. Because these homemade treats don't include preservatives, they have a short shelf life.

YIELDS: 30 (1") treats

2 ounces cream cheese

¼ pound sliced low-sodium turkey breast

1. Spread 1–2 tablespoons of cream cheese on a slice of turkey breast.

2. Roll up tightly, then slice into 1" pieces.

3. Refrigerate for up to 3 days, storing flat to keep the treats from unrolling.

Anchovy Bites

The strong-tasting anchovies in this recipe make this a tasty option for training treat nuggets. If you don't have anchovies on hand, sardines, another Fido fave, will work well, too.

YIELDS: 36 (2") treats

1 (2-ounce) can anchovies in olive oil (do not drain)

¼ cup water

1 egg

1½ cups rolled oats

1½ cups whole-wheat flour

4 teaspoons finely chopped parsley (fresh or dry)

1. Preheat oven to 350°F. Grease a cookie sheet or line with parchment paper.

2. In a blender, purée anchovies, water, and egg.

3. Mix oats, flour, and parsley in a large bowl. Add anchovy mixture and mix completely.

4. Use a melon baller or small scoop to make small balls of dough; place on cookie sheet.

5. Bake for 25–30 minutes until golden brown.

6. Cool completely before serving or refrigerating. Store in the refrigerator for 3 days or freeze in an airtight container for up to 6 months.

Liver Corn Bread

If you're at all squeamish about working with liver in dough, this recipe keeps your hands off the liver!

YIELDS: 48 (1") treats

1 pound beef or chicken liver, rinsed

1 (8.5-ounce) box corn muffin mix

1 egg

1. Preheat oven to 350°F. Grease a cookie sheet with at least a ½" edge.

2. In a blender, purée liver. Pour liver into a large mixing bowl. Add corn muffin mix and egg. Stir until just combined, then pour batter onto cookie sheet.

3. Bake for 30 minutes.

4. Cool before slicing, then refrigerate. Refrigerate for up to 3 days or freeze in an airtight container for up to 6 months.

······ **Where Do You Carry Your Treats?** ······

If you've ever watched the Westminster Kennel Club Dog Show on television, you've seen trainers holding treats in their cheeks to dispense to their dogs during the competition. Other trainers use pockets or small "bait bags" for keeping their cache of tasty morsels handy.

Oatmeal Turkey Dog Biscuits

Keep this recipe in mind when planning your holiday cooking schedule. That leftover turkey will be perfect for these easy-to-prepare biscuits! Your dogs will appreciate their "Thanksgiving" leftovers. If you don't have turkey, chicken will work just fine too.

YIELDS: 24 (2") biscuits

1¾ cups whole-wheat flour

2½ cups quick-cooking oats

1 teaspoon baking powder

1 cup turkey (or chicken) broth

1½ cups cooked shredded turkey (or chicken)

1. Preheat oven to 350°F. Grease two cookie sheets or line with parchment paper.

2. Mix dry ingredients in a large bowl and set aside. Add broth and turkey to a blender, then blend to the consistency of baby food. Add this meat mixture to the dry ingredients and mix well.

3. Turn out dough on a lightly floured surface and knead. This is a heavy dough, so it takes some muscle! Roll out the dough and cut into shapes; place on cookie sheets.

4. Bake for 25 minutes until the treats are golden brown.

5. Be sure to cool the biscuits completely before serving to your dog or refrigerating. Refrigerate for 3 days or freeze in an airtight container for up to 6 months.

Awesome Oatmeal

Oatmeal is a great source of soluble fiber for your dog and an excellent choice especially for senior dogs—or for any dog with wheat allergies. Unlike your own oatmeal, though, don't add any sugars or spices to your dog's oatmeal goodies.

Chicken and Cheese Biscuits

If your dog is sensitive to dairy, consider using goat cheese in these savory biscuits; many dogs that are lactose intolerant can still digest goat cheese. Also, compared to cow's milk cheese, cheeses made from goat's milk have a higher calcium content, encouraging bone density.

YIELDS: 24 (2") biscuits

1½ cups shredded, cooked chicken

¾ cup chicken broth, divided

½ cup shredded cheese, such as Cheddar, Romano, or goat cheese

1 cup whole-wheat flour

1 cup all-purpose flour

1. Preheat oven to 350°F. Grease two cookie sheets or line with parchment paper.

2. Purée chicken and ½ cup chicken broth in a blender or food processor until it is the consistency of baby food.

3. In a large separate bowl, mix cheese and flours, then add chicken/chicken broth mixture.

4. Slowly add a teaspoon of reserved broth at a time until the dough is the right consistency to knead.

5. Turn out dough on a lightly floured surface and knead; roll out the dough to about ¼" thickness. Cut with cookie cutters into 24 shapes, then place on cookie sheets.

6. Bake for 30 minutes, then remove from oven and allow the treats to cool completely on a drying rack before refrigerating or serving. Refrigerate for 5 days or freeze in an airtight container for up to 6 months.

Mini Cheeseburger Treats

Talk about tempting: What dog wouldn't like these meaty, cheesy, juicy favorites? If you prefer, ground turkey can also be substituted in this yummy treat recipe. The small cheeseburgers are also easy to break apart for training treat bits.

YIELDS: 24 treats

1 pound lean ground beef

½ cup shredded Cheddar cheese

1 egg

2 pieces toasted whole-wheat sandwich bread, crushed

1. Preheat oven to 350°F. Spray mini-cupcake tins or line with parchment cups.

2. In a large mixing bowl, combine all ingredients by hand and knead mixture until the bread is worked throughout the mix.

3. Pinch off 1" balls of mixture, roll into balls, and drop into the greased cupcake pan, pressing lightly to pack mix into mold.

4. Bake for 30 minutes and remove from oven. Remove mini cheeseburgers from the cupcake pans and allow them to cool on paper towels or a drying rack.

5. Cool completely before refrigerating or serving. Refrigerate for 3 days or freeze in an airtight container for up to 6 months.

Carrot and Cheese Biscuits

Not just for rabbits, carrots are a great canine food, whether in meals, treats, or in raw form. Low in calories and high in fiber, carrots are rich in beta carotene (a natural antioxidant), and dogs love their sweet taste.

YIELDS: 24 (2") biscuits

1 cup shredded carrots

1 cup shredded cheese, such as Cheddar or Monterey Jack

1 tablespoon extra-virgin olive oil

2¾ cups whole-wheat flour

2 cups bran cereal, crushed (do *not* use bran flakes with raisins)

2 teaspoons baking powder

1½ cups water

1. Preheat oven to 350°F. Grease two cookie sheets or line with parchment paper.

2. Mix carrots, cheese, and oil in a large bowl; in a smaller bowl, mix dry ingredients. Add dry ingredients to the carrot mixture, then add water, mixing well.

3. Pinch off a golf ball–size piece of dough, drop onto cookie sheet, and slightly flatten with a fork. Repeat until all dough is used.

4. Bake for 25 minutes until browned. Cool completely before serving or refrigerating. Refrigerate for 5 days or freeze in an airtight container for up to 6 months.

Why Is My Bone Orange?

As with other vegetables, dogs are unable to break down the cellulose walls of raw carrots, so they can't absorb all the nutrients. Raw carrots are helpful in cleaning your dog's teeth, though; they help to scrape plaque from the tooth surface without the risk of a broken tooth (as with bones).

CHAPTER 6

Frozen Treats

Looking for a way to cool your canine during the dog days of summer? Frozen treats can cool and treat your dog all at once. Many dogs enjoy the crunching of frozen treats, while others need the treat to warm slightly to better take in the aroma of the frozen goodie. Frozen treats are also excellent for keeping your dog busy, especially if he's experiencing separation anxiety or boredom. A frozen treat given just before you head to work can occupy your dog for a while in your absence, or keep him busy while you tend to that important phone call. Stuffable toys like KONG® rubber toys can be filled with liquid mixtures and frozen; their shape will slow your dog's chewing to extend the life of the treat and to reduce choking hazards.

Mango Sorbet GF P R

Is your dog lactose intolerant? This yummy dairy-free dessert makes a great ice cream substitute for you and your dog! The national fruit of India, the mango has long been used in Ayurvedic medicine and, although there are many varieties of mangos, all pack a powerful nutritional punch. Fat free, sodium free, and cholesterol free, the fruit contains more than twenty different vitamins and minerals.

YIELDS: 2 cups, or 28 ice cubes

2 ripe mangos, peeled

Juice of 1 orange

Juice of 1 lime

½ cup unsweetened almond milk

1. Add all ingredients to a blender and purée.
2. Pour mixture into an ice cube tray.
3. Freeze overnight. When frozen, transfer cubes to a zip-top plastic bag to store up to 2 months in the freezer.

What Kind of Cow Makes Almond Milk?

Lactose-intolerant dogs (or people) will find almond milk an easy substitute. Homemade almond milk (the most Paleo-friendly choice) is made by puréeing ground nuts and water, or you can buy a commercial version. Either can be used as a milk substitute—it has a creamy texture and somewhat nutty taste.

Raw Puppy Pops®

These little nuggets of flavor and nutrition are sure to please, whether as a training reward or just as a healthy snack. Alfalfa sprouts are a super-concentrated source of vitamins A and C, chelated minerals, plant proteins, fiber, and other nutrients.

YIELDS: About 50 (1") treats

1 pound raw lean ground turkey, lamb, or beef

¼ cup chopped fresh parsley

¼ cup chopped alfalfa sprouts

¼ cup sesame seeds

1. Combine meat, parsley, and sprouts in a bowl.

2. Pinch off a small portion and roll into a 1" ball. Roll in sesame seeds. Place on a cookie sheet. Repeat until all ingredients are used.

3. When all the mixture has been portioned, place cookie sheet in freezer for a few hours until frozen. Once frozen, bag treats in zip-top bags to dispense frozen or thawed. They can be stored for up to 6 months in the freezer.

Hiring a Veterinary Nutritionist

Would you like a homemade diet formulated especially for your dog by a veterinary nutritionist? Veterinary nutritionists are "diplomates" of the American College of Veterinary Nutrition (ACVN) and can help formulate a balanced homemade diet. You'll find veterinary nutritionists listed in the ACVN Diplomate Directory at *www.acvn.org*.

Raw Dog Treats GF P R

These small frozen snacks are an easy raw treat. Slightly thawed, they also offer a good solution for dispensing pills to your dog, even if you don't feed a raw diet.

YIELDS: 30 (1") treats

1 pound ground sirloin

1 egg

2 tablespoons molasses

1 cup finely chopped raw pumpkin seeds

1. Line a cookie sheet with parchment paper.

2. Mix sirloin, egg, and molasses in a large bowl.

3. Pour out chopped raw pumpkin seeds on a separate piece of parchment paper.

4. Use a small cookie or ice cream scoop or pinch off small amounts and shape meat mixture into 1" balls. Roll sirloin balls in chopped pumpkin seeds to coat.

5. Place balls on cookie sheet, then freeze overnight.

6. Once frozen, remove balls from cookie sheet and store, frozen, in zip-top plastic bags. Freeze for up to 6 months.

Brothsicles GF P

This easy frozen treat is a good way to encourage your dog to consume extra water on hot days!

YIELDS: 30 servings

12 cups water

1 pound chicken meat

1. Add water and chicken meat to a 4-quart (or larger) slow cooker. Cook chicken on low overnight in the slow cooker, at least 8 hours. If using whole chicken parts, remove the bones and skin from the mix and discard. When done, shred any large pieces and return the chicken to the slow cooker.

2. Stir the mixture. Ladle the broth mixture into plastic cups or ice cube trays. Chicken will settle to the bottom of the broth, so stir between each Brothsicle so each frozen treat includes bits of chicken.

3. Freeze overnight. When frozen, store in a zip-top plastic bag in the freezer for up to 6 months.

How Much Water Should Dogs Drink?

Dehydration is a scary, and sometimes life-threatening, condition. Dogs need almost 1 ounce of water per pound of their body weight daily. That means an 8-pound Papillon needs 1 cup, while an 80-pound Lab will need 2½ quarts per day—and more if they're hot or active.

Fido's Frozen Fruit Pupsicles ®℗

Blueberries and strawberries are popular with most dogs, while others enjoy melons, peaches, and apples. This recipe is easy to customize for your dog's favorite fruits. These pupsicles have molasses for added sweetness and nutrition; some dogs are a bit reluctant to eat some fruits at first. If you don't want to add the extra sugar of the molasses (since the fruit contains sugars), just omit it.

YIELDS: 56 ice cubes

1 cup cored and diced fresh fruit (*not* grapes or raisins)

4 cups water

1 tablespoon blackstrap molasses (optional)

1 In a large bowl, mix fruit with water and molasses, if using.

2 Freeze the mix in ice cube trays or small tubs. When frozen, store in a zip-top plastic bag in the freezer for up to 6 months.

Pits Are the Pits!

Always discard peach pits; they're toxic to dogs if they chew on them, as are the pits of other fruit, such as apricots and plums. If you use apples, discard the seeds for the same reason.

Beefsicle Frozen Dog Treats GF

It's always important to keep your dog well-hydrated during the summer months. All your dog will know is that he's getting a tasty, cool treat with this easy-to-make Beefsicle.

YIELDS: 35–40 servings

1 pound ground beef

1 cup peas (fresh, canned, or frozen)

7 cups water, divided

1. Place ground beef, peas, and 2 cups of water in a blender or food processor.

2. Mix on low, then increase the speed to purée the mixture. Add 1 cup water and continue to liquefy.

3. Continue to liquefy for 1–2 minutes; this will spin off much of the fat of the ground beef. (You'll see a white film of fat building up on the inside of the blender.)

4. Pour the mixture into a 10-quart saucepan. Discard fat clinging to the blender.

5. Add remaining 4 cups water. Cook on high until the water reaches a boil, then reduce the heat to medium and allow it to cook at a slow boil for 30 minutes.

6. Remove from heat.

7. After the mixture has cooled completely, pour mixture into plastic tubs or ice cube trays. Freeze overnight. Store in an airtight container for up to 6 months in a zip-top bag in the freezer.

Peanut Butter and Banana Dog Ice Cream GF

You can find doggie ice cream in the freezer section of your grocery store, but it's also very easy (and inexpensive) to make at home. With our long Texas summers, we are always looking for ways to cool down our pooches!

YIELDS: About 50 servings

3–4 ripe bananas

4 cups low-fat plain yogurt

½ cup organic unsweetened peanut butter

1. Peel bananas and add to a blender along with yogurt and peanut butter.

2. Blend until smooth, then pour into ice cube trays.

3. Freeze and serve frozen. Freeze in an airtight container for up to 6 months.

The Plainer, the Better

Plain yogurt is always the best choice for dogs because it doesn't include the added sugars of flavored yogurts. Also, to ramp up the nutritional value, watch for yogurt made from the milk of grass-fed cows, which contains more conjugated linoleic acid (a fatty acid that's credited with anti-cancer and weight-management properties), and organic yogurt (to avoid added hormones).

Watermelon Slush GF R

Low-calorie watermelon is a tasty and nutritious way to cool off during the dog days of summer. Packed with potassium and magnesium, plus vitamins A and C, watermelon also helps prevent dehydration because it is filled with fluid.

YIELDS: 4 cups, or about 56 ice cubes

2 cups cubed seedless watermelon

½ cup strawberries, hulled

1 tablespoon molasses

½ cup coconut water

1 cup ice

1. Combine all ingredients in a blender and mix.
2. Serve in a bowl as a slushie treat, or pour into a KONG® and freeze for long-lasting cooling fun.

Share a Slice of Fun

Many dogs love plain watermelon slices. Be sure your dog doesn't eat the seeds or rind—but otherwise, feel free to share your summer slice with him!

Pumpkin Ice Cream GF R

You may be tempted to compete with your canine for this delish frozen delight. Super simple to make, it's nutritious, too.

YIELDS: 2½ cups, or about 36 ice cubes

1 cup Pumpkin Purée (see Chapter 15)

1 cup low-fat plain yogurt

½ cup organic unsweetened peanut butter

1. Combine all ingredients in a blender, then pour into ice cube trays.

2. Freeze and serve frozen. Freeze in an airtight container for up to 6 months.

Blueberry Pops GF R

Along with serving as small treats, this ice cream also makes a fun filling for a stuffable, rubber, treat-dispensing toy for some longer-lasting fun.

YIELDS: 2 cups, or about 28 ice cubes

1 cup blueberries

1 cup low-fat plain yogurt

1. Purée blueberries and yogurt in a blender.
2. Pour in ice cube trays and freeze. Serve frozen. Freeze in an airtight container for up to 6 months.

Washing Fresh Produce

To be sure you get rid of any bacteria and pesticides used on fruit, the best way to wash berries is to give them a good rinse under cold running water right before use.

Bacon Ice Cream GF

Everything's better with bacon, right? It's higher in fat than fruit ice cream, but a cube of Bacon Ice Cream makes a nice reward after a training class, a vet visit, or a nail trim.

YIELDS: 1½ cups, or about 22 ice cubes

1 cup low-fat plain yogurt

3 bacon slices, cooked and finely crumbled

1 teaspoon bacon fat

1. In a large bowl, mix all ingredients. Pour into ice cube trays and freeze.

2. Freeze in an airtight container for up to 6 months.

Bacon Mania

The last decade has seen a boom in all things bacon, but our dogs have long held a love for this porky product. While humans may get creative with novelties like candied bacon, chicken-fried bacon, and chocolate-covered bacon, dogs know that simpler is better.

CHAPTER 7

Jerky and Chews

In the last few years, numerous dog deaths and illnesses have been attributed to tainted jerky chews made with ingredients from China. There's absolutely no need to put your dog's health or your own peace of mind at risk, though, because it's super easy to make your own healthy jerky and chews for your dog. You'll know just how the chews were prepared, and you'll know they were created with human-grade ingredients.

Homemade jerky chews also have the advantage of letting you customize the thickness and chewiness of the chew based on your own dog. If you have a senior who is missing some teeth, create a softer chew. If you're sharing your home with a young chewing machine, create a tougher chew. Even better—you can make them all for a fraction of the price you'd pay for chews in the store.

Dried Beef Strips GF P

Skirt steak (often used for making fajitas) is an inexpensive choice for this tasty treat. While its toughness requires marinating for fajitas, that same toughness makes this cut a great choice for a chew.

**YIELDS: 10–20 treats,
½" × 6"**

1 pound skirt steak

1. Preheat oven to 300°F. Line a cookie sheet with parchment paper.

2. Slice beef into narrow strips no wider than ½". Place strips on the cookie sheet, but do not allow strips to touch.

3. Bake for 1 hour, then lower oven temperature to 200°F. Open oven door slightly so moisture will escape the oven. Continue to bake the strips for 2 hours.

4. Remove strips from oven and place on a wire drying rack until completely cooled.

5. Refrigerate portions. Store for up to 3 days in the refrigerator or freeze up to 6 months.

.... **Deep Freeze** ....

It's easy to have healthy treats on hand when you cook a large quantity and store them in your freezer—but for how long? According to the U.S. Food and Drug Administration, freezing at 0°F keeps food safe indefinitely but the quality of the food may change after a certain period. Food stored for long periods will remain safe, but if you're sharing it with your dog, you may notice a change in texture or flavor after a 4- to 6-month period for most foods. Regardless of freezer time, it's always important to use airtight storage to avoid freezer burn.

Liver Logs GF

Stuffed celery stalks provide a healthy chew for dogs to enjoy without the calories of rawhides and other chew sticks.

YIELDS: 10–15 treats

8 ounces cream cheese

½ pound chicken liver, rinsed

2 tablespoons olive oil

1 head celery

1. Remove cream cheese from refrigerator and let it soften while preparing liver.

2. In a medium skillet, fry liver in olive oil until liver is no longer pink. Remove from heat and use a fork to break up the liver as much as possible.

3. In a mixing bowl, use a fork or hand mixer to combine cream cheese and chicken liver. Mix until no large pieces of liver are visible.

4. Wash celery and trim ends. Fill with cream cheese–liver mixture, either with a fork or by piping it using a plastic bag with the corner snipped off. Each treat is one stalk of celery (no need to trim off leaves). Refrigerate up to 3 days.

Dehydrated Chicken Liver Treats GF P

If you don't have a dehydrator, you can make these in the oven on its lowest temperature setting, baking on a lightly greased cookie sheet, and flipping the chicken livers after about 2 hours.

YIELDS: 20–30 treats

1 pound chicken liver, rinsed

1. Spray the dehydrator trays with nonstick spray.

2. If any livers are too thick, use a fork to flatten them slightly.

3. Lay out livers on dehydrator trays, leaving space between them so there will be good air circulation throughout the trays.

4. Allow livers to dehydrate, check drying level periodically.

5. When livers are noticeably dryer, swap position of drying trays and allow to further dehydrate, roughly 4 hours. (Drying times will vary with model of dehydrator.)

6. Once done, allow the chicken livers to cool, then store them in the refrigerator for up to 1 week (although they didn't last anywhere near that long here . . . our dogs loved them!) or freeze in an airtight container for up to 6 months.

Dehydrated Sweet Potato Chews GF P

Dehydrated sweet potatoes make a healthy and tasty chew that's a safe substitute for rawhide. If you don't have a food dehydrator, these dehydrated treats can also be prepared in the oven at 250°F for 3 hours.

YIELDS: 18–25 chews,
¼" × 3"

2 medium sweet potatoes

1. Wash and peel the sweet potatoes, being careful to remove any sprouts or green spots.

2. Slice the potatoes lengthwise no thinner than ¼" thickness. Slightly thicker slices will be chewier for your dog (although they won't dry out as well and will have a shorter shelf life, even in the refrigerator).

3. Arrange the slices on the dehydrating trays. Don't allow the slices to touch one another or the edges won't dry properly.

4. Dry the potatoes for about 14 hours (although this will vary by dehydrator).

5. Cool and refrigerate. Refrigerate up to 1 week or freeze in an airtight container for up to 6 months.

·········· **Avoid the Evil Eye!** ··········

The green parts of sprouted potatoes contain solanine, a glycoalkaloid poison. It's toxic not only to dogs but also to people (although poisoning is rare because of the bitter taste). Avoiding it is simple, though; just discard any green or sprouted part of the potato!

Turkey Jerky Treats GF P

Unlike jerky for humans, doggie jerky is mild and generally unseasoned. Dehydrating the jerky makes it stay fresh longer (although your dog may have other ideas!) and makes it easier to put in your pocket as a training treat. Remember that you'll need *many* training treats when initially training your dog, so the key is first to make training treats very small (pea-size) and compensate by reducing your dog's meal size as well. Low-sodium soy sauce or blackstrap molasses can be substituted for teriyaki sauce. Dogs also love the flavor of the turkey alone.

YIELDS: About 50 (6") treats

2 pounds lean ground turkey

2 tablespoons teriyaki sauce (optional)

1. Preheat oven to 170°F.

2. Fill jerky gun (see sidebar) with ground turkey and slowly squeeze out jerky onto baking screens with drip trays underneath them.

3. Bake for 2 hours.

4. Turn each of the pieces, then cook for 30 minutes more. Cool completely before refrigerating. These can be cut into training treat–size portions as well! Refrigerate for up to 3 days or freeze in an airtight container for up to 6 months.

What's a Jerky Gun?

A jerky gun can make preparing treats from processed ingredients quicker and easier. These kitchen tools typically cost between $25 and $40 and allow you to squeeze out uniform amounts of the mixture by pulling the trigger, much like a cake decorating gun.

Chicken Jerky GF P

Numerous recalls of chicken jerky chews in recent years have understandably alarmed dog lovers. Along with omitting preservatives and other additives, creating your own easy-to-make chicken jerky gives you quality control over your dog's snacks.

YIELDS: 12 strips, ¼" × 4"

1 pound chicken breasts, deboned

1. Preheat oven to 170°F or lowest temperature setting.

2. Lightly grease a cookie sheet. (Use one with a small edge because there will be water and juices running from the chicken during the first hour of cooking.)

3. Slice chicken breasts in strips no more than ¼" thick. Place slices on cookie sheet, leaving at least ½" between slices.

4. Bake for 2 hours. After 2 hours, check the slices and see if they're dry.

5. Continue baking until slices appear very dried.

6. When done, remove the treats from the oven and cool on a drying rack.

7. When the treats are completely cool, bag in zip-top bags or place in an airtight container. Refrigerate for 3 days or freeze for up to 6 months.

Superior Slicing

It's easiest to slice the chicken breasts if they're slightly frozen. Slice with the grain of the chicken, rather than against it, to make the treats a little chewier for your dog.

Dehydrated Beet Chips GF P

**These chewy chips make a healthy option for dogs
who love to gnaw on their treats!**

**YIELDS: About 2 cups, or
25 chips**

1 pound fresh beets

Nonstick cooking spray or
olive oil, as needed

1. Preheat oven to 350°F. Line a cookie sheet with parchment paper.

2. Wash and peel beets. Remove stems. Slice beets ¼" thick. (In a rush? Buy a can of low-sodium sliced beets. Drain and rinse the beets before baking.) Spray beets lightly with cooking spray or olive oil.

3. Place beet slices on parchment paper with no edges touching.

4. Bake for 30–40 minutes. Turn off oven and allow beets to remain in oven for 10 additional minutes, then remove and cool on a wire rack.

5. Cool completely before serving or refrigerating. Store in the refrigerator for 5 days or freeze in an airtight container for up to 6 months.

Beets Are Neat (and Nutritious)

Beets are filled with beta carotene, fiber, iron, potassium, and magnesium, as well as vitamins A, B, and C. Especially recommended for dogs with liver illnesses, beets are a great boost to any dog for their detoxifying qualities.

Dehydrated Juice Pulp Treats (GF)

Looking for a way to use the pulp left after juicing your favorite fruits and vegetables? Turn them into irresistible treats for your pooch!

YIELDS: About 30 (2") treats

½ cup ground flaxseed

1 cup water

1 cup sunflower seeds, chopped peanuts, or your dog's favorite nuts

1 tablespoon blackstrap molasses

4 cups pulp from dog-safe fruits and vegetables (see lists in Chapter 1)

1. Soak ground flaxseed in water for at least 30 minutes. Drain.

2. Preheat oven to lowest setting. Line two cookie sheets with parchment paper.

3. Mix flaxseed, seeds or nuts, molasses, and pulp, then spread on parchment-lined cookie sheets to about ¼" thickness.

4. Bake sheets for about 12 hours until treats are crunchy and dry.

5. Cool completely before serving or storing. Store in the refrigerator for 5 days or freeze in an airtight container for up to 6 months.

CHAPTER 8

Training Treats

We love positive reinforcement training, and our dogs do, too! Training is part of our daily lives with our dogs; they receive pea-size bits for good behavior and for responding to a request. We alternate treats with praise, and sometimes give a "jackpot" of several treats so they never know quite what to expect (much like a person at a slot machine!). The key to making training treats is to find a treat that's easy to break into small pieces (because you will be using many each day) and using strong-smelling meat. Meat-based training treats are more successful with most dogs; warming them in your pocket or hand will make them even more tempting!

Cheese and Garlic Training Treats

Always be sure to use garlic powder, never garlic salt, in dog treat recipes. The strong smell of the garlic makes these quite appealing as training treats.

YIELDS: 25 (2") treats

1 cup whole-wheat flour

1 cup grated Cheddar cheese

1 tablespoon garlic powder

1 tablespoon butter, softened

½ cup milk

1. Preheat oven to 350°F. Grease a cookie sheet or line with parchment paper.

2. In a large bowl, mix all ingredients except the milk by hand. Slowly add in the milk a bit at a time, and mix until all ingredients are combined.

3. Turn out dough on a floured surface and knead; roll out the dough to ¼" thickness.

4. Cut dough with your favorite cookie cutters and place on cookie sheet. Bake for 15 minutes or until golden brown.

5. To make treats extra crispy, turn off the oven, crack the oven door a bit, and allow the treats to cool completely in the oven.

6. Refrigerate for 5 days or freeze in an airtight container for up to 6 months.

··········· **Garlic: Good or Not?** ···········

Garlic is a member of the same family as the onion, a food you should never serve to dogs. Garlic, too, can lead to anemia when eaten in large doses. Talk with your veterinarian about safe levels for your dog.

Canine Crouton Treats

Wondering what to do with that stale bread? Croutons are easy to make for you and your dog; add 1 teaspoon of garlic powder to your portion if you like them spicy.

YIELDS: 60 (1") square croutons

6 slices whole-wheat bread

½ cup grated Parmesan cheese

½ cup melted bacon fat or olive oil

1. Preheat oven to 250°F.

2. Use kitchen shears to cut bread into 1" squares.

3. In a medium bowl, add Parmesan cheese and toss the bread squares with cheese. Drizzle bread with fat or oil while continuing to toss the bread so all the cubes are coated.

4. Spread croutons on a cookie sheet and bake for 30–40 minutes. Turn the croutons midway through baking to brown evenly.

5. Remove croutons from the oven and allow them to cool before refrigerating or serving. Refrigerate for 5 days or freeze in an airtight container for up to 6 months.

Beef Heart Treats GF P

Beef heart is considered a muscle meat, not an organ (which is important because only 10 percent of your dog's diet should be organ meat), and it makes a healthy and economical treat or meal. It can be found in most grocery stores, either sold whole or as a half heart.

YIELDS: 40 (½") treats

1 pound beef heart

2 tablespoons olive oil

1 tablespoon garlic powder (optional)

1. Cube the meat in small chunks. In a large skillet, fry chunks in olive oil over medium-high heat for about 10 minutes.

2. Sprinkle with garlic powder if you choose.

3. Refrigerate for 3 days or freeze in an airtight container for up to 6 months.

We "Heart" Heart!

Beef heart doesn't have the panache of sirloin or rib eye, but this muscle meat is an excellent option for dogs and humans. If you can't handle working with the entire heart, you can purchase a half heart or ask your butcher to slice it for you. Besides getting an economical cut of meat, you'll know you are using a cut that otherwise might be discarded.

Liver Training Treats

Liver makes a flavorful and motivating training treat for most dogs! Chicken liver can also be substituted here. These treats can be broken into pea-size bits to use in dog training.

YIELDS: 45 (½"-square) training treats

1 pound raw organic beef liver, rinsed

2 cups whole-wheat flour

1 egg

½ cup water

1. Preheat oven to 350°F.

2. Purée liver in a blender or food processor.

3. In a mixing bowl, pour the liver purée and mix with flour, egg, and water. Stir well. The result is a heavy batter. Pour batter onto a well-greased cookie sheet (one with a good lip). This mix won't rise much at all.

4. Bake for 30 minutes. Remove cookie sheet from oven and score the treats into ½" squares.

5. Return the cookie sheet with the scored treats back to the oven for about 10 minutes to dry out treats. After 10 minutes, turn off oven, flip treats again, and return the cookie sheet to the oven. Leave treats in oven until the oven cools.

6. When removing from oven, if treats are not completely cooled, let them cool on a drying rack before serving or refrigerating. Refrigerate for 3 days or freeze in an airtight container for up to 6 months.

Meat Is Sweeter for Treats

Meat (rather than sweet) treats are the most effective training treats with many dogs; often, the stronger-scented treats like liver are best.

Chicken Liver Squares GF P

This easy recipe makes a good base for stuffable dog-treat dispensers. Use it as the "plug" in the treat-dispensing toy, then fill the toy with chopped celery, green beans, green peas, or your dog's favorite fruit.

YIELDS: 50 (1") squares

1 pound chicken

3 eggs

1 pound chicken liver, rinsed

1. Preheat oven to 220°F. Lightly grease two cookie sheets or line with parchment paper.

2. Add chicken and eggs to a blender or food processor. Add chicken liver to mixture, pouring all juices into mixture. Purée.

3. Pour mixture in the centers of the two cookie sheets, then bake. After 1 hour, cut each mixture into 1" squares and flip so that all sides of the treats will brown. Bake for 1 more hour.

4. When treats are browned, turn off the oven but leave the cookie sheets in the heated oven to cool for several hours.

5. Cool treats completely before serving or refrigerating. Refrigerate or freeze all treats. Refrigerate for 3 days or freeze in an airtight container for up to 6 months.

Hot Dog Training Treats GF

These treats may not be the ritziest, but for training purposes, you can't beat these bits of all-American motivation. All-beef or turkey hot dogs are the best choice, and for extra points, you can use organic hot dogs to make these tasty treats.

YIELDS: About 100 training treats

1 package (10) all-beef hot dogs

1. Slice each hot dog into 10 pieces.

2. Place hot dog medallions on about six layers of plain paper towels.

3. Microwave hot dogs on the paper towels for 5 minutes. Cooking times will vary by microwave.

4. Blot grease from top of hot dogs and turn; microwave for an additional 2–3 minutes. When some hot dogs begin to darken around the edges, they are done.

5. Cool completely before serving. Refrigerate for 5 days or freeze in an airtight container for up to 6 months.

The Lowdown on Hot Dogs

Hot dogs are powerful motivators for most dogs and are a favorite with many trainers. You can use organic beef or turkey hot dogs, or regular all-beef or turkey hot dogs; regardless of the variety, check that the hot dogs do not include onion powder. It's true that some hot dogs are made from less-than-desirable animal parts, so look for premium brands made from select cuts.

CHAPTER 9

Stuffers

This section contains treats that can be stuffed into a stuffable toy like a KONG® to extend the fun of the treat. A natural alternative is to use a hollow marrow bone. Never use a cooked marrow bone; these are far too dry and you'll run the risk of splintering, which can be dangerous and even deadly if your dog ingests shards of bone. Newer marrow bones that haven't completely dried out work best for this purpose. If you use a commercial stuffing toy like a KONG®, be sure to clean it after each treating session. These toys can be washed in the upper rack of the dishwasher so you're ready for the next treating session; they're also freezable to make the stuffing last longer.

Pigskin Surprise GF P

Stuff your dog's favorite treat-dispensing toy with this easy mix. It can also be frozen to last longer.

YIELDS: Fills 1 large KONG®

1 ounce cream cheese

1 cup plain chicharrónes or pork rinds

1 egg

1. Using a clean KONG® or other treat-dispensing toy, plug the small end of the toy with a small portion of the cream cheese. (Other options include peanut butter or soft bread.)

2. Mix chicharrónes or pork rinds and raw egg in a bowl, breaking rinds slightly so they're saturated by egg. (If you are concerned about raw eggs, cook to semi-firm consistency and cool before serving.)

3. Add mixture to toy until filled. Plug larger opening of the toy with remaining cream cheese.

Frozen KONG® GF

The rubber KONG® toy is a favorite with trainers and behaviorists as a way to keep dogs busy and distracted. A frozen KONG® is a great way to provide a long-lasting treat on a summer day; your dog won't be able to quickly break the ice with his teeth and will have to resort to licking the treat from the rubber toy.

YIELDS: Fills 1 large KONG®

1 KONG®

1 coffee mug

1 cup Beef Stock (see Chapter 15)

1. To freeze the KONG®, which has an opening at each end, place the toy inside a coffee mug with the small opening at the bottom of the cup.

2. Pour the stock into the toy; freeze until solid. Remove toy from cup before serving.

············· **Fun Frozen Meals** ·················

A frozen KONG® can also be used to serve meals, especially helpful for gulping dogs or dogs that need to be occupied. Add meat and vegetables to the Beef Stock before freezing.

King KONG®

Since the size of KONG® toys varies by the size of your dog, adjust this recipe for your own dog. You can also use this to stuff marrow bones.

YIELDS: Fills 1 medium KONG®

1 tablespoon organic unsweetened peanut butter

1 KONG®

1 medium banana, mashed

1 tablespoon low-fat plain yogurt

1. Use half of the peanut butter to plug the small end of the KONG®.

2. In a small bowl, stir banana and yogurt together, then fill KONG®. Use remaining peanut butter to plug the larger opening.

3. Serve frozen or at room temperature.

Anxiety? Just Stuff It!

If your dog suffers from separation anxiety or boredom, a stuffable toy makes a great diversion. Freeze the toy to make the fun last longer and mix up the goodies inside: meats, cooked rice, mashed potatoes, oatmeal, scrambled eggs, and any of your dog's favorite meals. For an added layer of fun, you could hide the loaded toy where your dog is unlikely to find it immediately, such as under a bed or, if outside, perhaps behind a hedge in the backyard. This works especially well with KONG® toys stuffed with dry ingredients that aren't likely to melt or spoil.

Sardine Stuffing GF R

You might picture cats when you think of sardines as a pet food, but dogs love this flavorful fish as well. Sardines are a healthy addition to treats, and are rich in omega-3 fatty acids, vitamin D, and phosphorus.

**YIELDS: 2 cups
(fills 2 medium KONG® toys)**

1 (3.75-ounce) can sardines in water (do not drain)

½ cup cottage cheese

½ cup plain Greek yogurt

1. In a blender, mix all ingredients until well blended.

2. Use as stuffing for a KONG® or other stuffable toy, or as a tasty topping for a main meal.

3. Refrigerate unused portion. Store in the refrigerator for 3 days or freeze in the KONG® for a longer-lasting treat.

·········· **Keeping the KONG® Stuffed** ··········

The key to keeping those KONG® toys stuffed—and making the toy/treat last longer for your dog—is a plug in both ends of the toys. A KONG® is made with a small hole in the top of the toy and a larger opening in the bottom. Some good options for plugging the holes include cream cheese, raw hamburger, peanut butter, cubes of cheese, or a slice of processed cheese.

Doggie Chopped Liver GF

Wondering what to do with those leftover hard-boiled Easter eggs? Make Doggie Chopped Liver! This recipe is an excellent way to plug a KONG® (however, since liver shouldn't make up more than 5 percent of your dog's diet, it shouldn't be used to actually stuff the entire KONG®). Along with its role as a KONG® plug, you can also use a tablespoon of doggie chopped liver to hide a pill, to reward your dog after a nail trim, or as a tasty topper on his evening meal.

YIELDS: About 1 pound filling

1 quart water

1 pound chicken liver, rinsed

2–3 hardboiled eggs, finely chopped

1. In a large pot, heat water to a boil. Add chicken livers (including juices) to boiling water; reduce heat and simmer for 40 minutes. Remove from heat.

2. Drain liver and reserve liquid for another use. (It's great for freezing in ice cube trays as a cool treat!)

3. Use a fork or potato masher to mash livers. Add eggs to livers. Mix well.

4. Use mixture as a plug for a KONG® or other stuffable toy, scooping a pea-size bit in the smaller opening of the toy and a tablespoon of the mixture in the larger opening. In between, use a medley of your dog's favorite veggies: green beans, celery, spinach, sweet potatoes, peas, and more. Refrigerate unused portion for up to 3 days, or freeze in an airtight container for up to 6 months.

Hold the Onions, Please!

Unlike traditional chopped liver, Doggie Chopped Liver has *no* onions. (Remember: onions are toxic to dogs and should never be included in their food or treats.)

CHAPTER 10

Holiday and Special Occasion Fun

Holidays are for all members of the family—both two- and four-legged! In this chapter, you'll find a selection of holiday recipes that use whole foods that you already purchase for traditional holiday dishes, from turkey to cranberries to pumpkin, to create treats for your dog.

As with our own holiday celebrations, the trick to successfully enjoying holiday foods is never to overindulge. Sadly, Thanksgiving is one of the busiest days at many emergency veterinary clinics, as dogs overeat on fats, gravies, and turkey skin, resulting in pancreatitis. Feeding your dog in moderation, always mindful of your dog's size, age, and activity level, is key to enjoying the holidays and making joyous memories.

Valentine Red Bell Pepper Cookies

Red bell peppers are a surprising favorite for many dogs, including our Irie, who has developed a taste for several different fruits and vegetables. Bell peppers don't produce capsaicin, so they're not hot like others in the pepper family.

YIELDS: About 18 (3") cookies

½ red bell pepper

¼ cup Homemade Chicken Broth (see Chapter 15)

2 eggs

2 tablespoons low-fat plain yogurt

2 teaspoons extra-virgin olive oil

3½ cups rice flour

½ cup chopped, cooked chicken

1 cup minced carrots

1. Preheat oven to 350°F. Grease a cookie sheet.

2. Wash red bell pepper; remove and discard stem, core, and seeds. Dice.

3. In a large bowl, add broth, eggs, yogurt, and olive oil to flour; stir slowly. Add in chicken and vegetables, stirring until mixed.

4. Use a spoon or melon baller to divide dough into golf ball–size balls. Roll, then flatten with the back of a fork on greased cookie sheet.

5. Bake for 30 minutes. Cool completely on a drying rack, then refrigerate. Refrigerate for 3 days or freeze in an airtight container for up to 6 months.

.... **Green versus Red Peppers** ....

You can substitute green bell peppers for red, but red peppers contain twice the vitamin C of green peppers. They also provide dogs much higher levels of carotene and lycopene.

St. Patty's Day Patties

For the Labs and Lassies in your home! This recipe relies on green peas to impart a greenish hue to the patties, but your dogs will appreciate the taste more than the appearance.

YIELDS: 30 (2") patties

1½ cups all-purpose flour

1 cup whole-wheat flour

2 teaspoons baking powder

4 strips bacon, diced

4 cups green peas, fresh or frozen

2 tablespoons water

1. Preheat oven to 325°F. Lightly oil a cookie sheet.

2. In a large bowl, mix dry ingredients. In a small skillet, fry bacon and reserve drippings; cool.

3. Place peas and water in a blender or food processor and purée. In a separate large bowl, mix blended peas and bacon with drippings; add dry ingredients and mix well.

4. Turn out dough on a lightly floured surface and knead; pat out or roll to under ½" thickness. Cut with cookie cutters to desired shape and place on lightly oiled cookie sheet.

5. Bake for 25 minutes or until browned.

6. Cool and serve or refrigerate. Refrigerate for 5 days or freeze in an airtight container for up to 6 months.

Easter Carrot Cake Cookies

The Easter bunny can come any time of year with these cookies that will leave Fido hopping for more! If your pooch is weight-challenged, you might want to ration him to one of these goodies a day. Remember: No more than 10 percent of his total diet should come from treats and goodies.

YIELDS: 28 (3") cookies

Cookies:

2 cups rolled oats

2 cups all-purpose flour

1 cup grated carrots

2 tablespoons molasses

8 tablespoons (½ cup) butter, softened

2 large eggs

2 teaspoons baking powder

½ cup water

Filling (optional):

4 ounces cream cheese, softened

1. Preheat oven to 350°F. Grease two cookie sheets or line with parchment paper.

2. In a large bowl, mix all ingredients except cream cheese; stir well until completely mixed.

3. Turn out dough on a lightly floured surface and roll to ¼" thickness. Cut into cookie shapes.

4. Bake for 30 minutes or until browned. Remove cookies from oven and cool completely.

5. After cookies are cooled, make some of them extra-special by turning them into a sandwich; layer some softened cream cheese between two cookies. Refrigerate for 5 days or freeze in an airtight container for up to 6 months.

Bowser's Brown Betty

Brown Betty is a traditional American dessert recipe. Much like a cobbler, the Brown Betty is based on fruit (traditionally apples) layered with a bread crumb crust.

YIELDS: 4 cups

8 tablespoons (½ cup) butter, divided

4 slices whole-wheat bread

4 apples, peeled and cored

1 tablespoon cinnamon

4 tablespoons blackstrap molasses

1. Preheat oven to 350°F. Grease a pie plate or 8" × 8" baking dish with half of the butter.

2. Cut bread into small pieces or crumble by hand. Cut apples into thin slices.

3. Alternate layers of bread and apples in the greased pie plate, then sprinkle with cinnamon. Drizzle with molasses and dot with slices of butter. Cover dish with foil.

4. Bake until golden brown (about 45 minutes).

5. Allow dog's portion to cool completely (although you can enjoy yours hot with a scoop of vanilla ice cream, if you like!). Refrigerate for 5 days or freeze in an airtight container for up to 6 months.

The Chef's Black Gold

Did you know a tablespoon of molasses contains the same amount of calcium as a glass of milk? Blackstrap molasses also supplies potassium, magnesium, vitamin B_6, selenium, manganese, iron, sulfur, and copper, making it a good choice for treat sweetening.

Witchy Chicken Fingers

This canine variation of the ever-popular Witches' Fingers cookie substitutes sugars and flavorings with savory chicken and the red decorating gel with plain old molasses.

YIELDS: 20 (½" × 4") cookies

1½ cups cooked chicken

1 egg

1 teaspoon baking powder

2 cups all-purpose flour

1½ cups whole-wheat flour

1 tablespoon molasses

20 whole almonds

1. Preheat oven to 350°F. Grease a cookie sheet.

2. In a blender, purée chicken to the consistency of baby food, adding a little water if necessary. Add egg and baking powder and mix.

3. In a medium bowl, add flours. Add puréed chicken mix to the flours and knead the dough.

4. Pinch off a golf ball–size piece of dough and roll it between your palms to make a tube of dough about 4" long. Roll it to about finger thickness, then place on cookie sheet.

5. Use the molasses to paint a little spot beneath the "fingernail" . . . it will ooze out from beneath the almond "nail" and look like blood. Place a single almond (the tip of the almond should be pointing out, like a spiky fingernail) and press down just a little to secure the almond in the dough.

6. Bake 20–25 minutes. Cool the treats completely before serving or refrigerating. Refrigerate for 3 days or freeze in an airtight container for up to 6 months.

Thanksgiving Frittata _{GF}

Wondering what to do with those Thanksgiving leftovers?
A frittata makes a meal for both you and your dog
that's easy to prepare and serve.

YIELDS: 6 servings

6 eggs

½ cup Pumpkin Purée (see Chapter 15)

2 tablespoons extra-virgin olive oil

½ cup chopped cooked green beans

1 cup chopped leftover turkey

1. In a large bowl, mix eggs and pumpkin. Set aside.

2. In a large skillet, heat olive oil over medium heat. Add turkey and green beans, heating thoroughly.

3. Reduce heat to medium-low. Pour in egg mixture over turkey and green beans. Cook until set, about 15 minutes.

4. Cool completely before serving your dog's portion. Refrigerate for 5 days or freeze in an airtight container for up to 6 months.

Turkey and Cranberry Treats

Wondering what to do with leftover turkey and cranberries? These treats combine Thanksgiving's most popular foods in a healthy and tasty treat.

YIELDS: 36 (2") treats

3½ cups whole-wheat flour

1 tablespoon baking powder

1 cup cooked, chopped turkey

1 tablespoon olive oil

1 egg

½ cup water or broth, as needed

1 cup whole cranberries

1. Preheat oven to 350°F. Lightly grease two cookie sheets.

2. In a large bowl, mix the flour and baking powder. In a blender or food processor, combine the turkey, olive oil, and egg (and some of the water or broth as needed). When the turkey is the consistency of baby food, add cranberries and continue to mix.

3. Pour this mixture into the mixing bowl with the dry ingredients and stir to create a thick dough.

4. On a lightly floured surface, knead the dough. (This is a heavy dough so you'll need to put a little muscle in it!)

5. Cut into biscuit shapes and place on cookie sheets. Bake for 25 minutes. Cool completely before serving or refrigerating. Refrigerate for 3 days or freeze in an airtight container for up to 6 months.

Fido's Fruitcake

Be sure to save one of these tasty treats for Santa! Although any fresh apples you may have on hand will work, some apple varieties are better than others for cooking. Look for Baldwin, Empire, Golden Delicious, or McIntosh, all excellent varieties.

YIELDS: 16 muffins

1 cup fresh cranberries

1 apple, peeled and cored

1 cup pecans or almonds, divided

2 cups all-purpose flour

⅓ cup molasses

1 egg

1 teaspoon baking powder

1 teaspoon cinnamon

1 cup water

1. Preheat oven to 350°F. Spray muffin tins or line with parchment cups.

2. Chop cranberries, apple, and half the nuts in a food processor or blender.

3. In a large bowl, combine all other ingredients; when mixed, add cranberry-apple-nut mixture and stir. Pour (heavy) batter into the muffin pans. Top with the remaining nuts.

4. Bake for 30 minutes, then cool completely before serving and refrigerating. Refrigerate for 5 days or freeze in an airtight container for up to 6 months.

Skip the Macadamias

If you don't have pecans or almonds, any other nut except macadamia nuts will work, too. (Macadamia nuts are toxic for dogs.) Peanuts are another popular option.

Bowser's Bacon Pretzels

These tasty pretzels are like an appetizer for a holiday gathering. Be warned: They're habit-forming!

YIELDS: 12 (5") treats

1 packet (2¼ teaspoons) active instant yeast

1½ cups warm water

1 teaspoon salt

1 tablespoon granulated sugar

4 cups all-purpose flour

1 pound thin-sliced bacon strips

1. Preheat oven to 425°F. Line a cookie sheet with parchment paper.

2. In a large bowl, dissolve yeast in warm water, stirring slowly. When dissolved, add salt and sugar.

3. Slowly add flour, 1 cup at a time, until dough is no longer sticky.

4. Turn dough out on a floured surface. Knead dough, then divide into 12 portions. Use palms of hands to form a rod with each portion.

5. Wrap each rod with a strip of bacon, spiraling down the rod to cover the entire treat. Place on cookie sheet.

6. Bake about 15 minutes, until the bread is cooked and the bacon is browned.

7. Cool completely before refrigerating or serving to dogs. Refrigerate for 3 days or freeze in an airtight container for up to 6 months.

Poochie Pumpkin Pupcakes

Cupcakes are all the rage now, and canine cupcakes are no exception! These are tasty just as they are, with no frosting, but they can be decorated for an extra-special touch.

YIELDS: 10 cupcakes

1 egg

1 teaspoon molasses

1 teaspoon baking soda

1 cup all-purpose flour

1 cup Pumpkin Purée (see Chapter 15)

4 tablespoons (¼ cup) butter, melted

1. Adjust oven rack to middle position. Preheat oven to 350°F.

2. Lightly grease a muffin tin or line with parchment cups.

3. In a medium bowl, combine all ingredients; mix thoroughly. Pour batter into prepared tin and bake for 30–35 minutes or until a toothpick inserted in the center of a cupcake comes out clean.

4. Remove from oven and transfer cupcakes to cool on a wire rack. Cool completely before frosting or serving. Refrigerate for 5 days or freeze in an airtight container for up to 6 months.

Frostings for Fido

Our dogs love their pupcakes undecorated, but if you'd like to add an extra-special touch, try the Mashed Potato Icing (see recipe in this chapter), or make a super-simple one-ingredient icing. Peanut butter makes an easy icing, as does cream cheese, low-fat plain yogurt, or cottage cheese.

Mashed Potato Icing GF

Make a special occasion even more special by icing a tasty dog biscuit or cupcake. This healthy icing can be used in place of traditional white sugar-based icing.

YIELDS: 2 cups

2 medium potatoes

2 tablespoons chopped fresh parsley

2 quarts water

2 tablespoons sour cream

1. Wash and peel potatoes, paying special attention to remove and discard any green portions of the potato. Cube potatoes and place in a large saucepan. Add parsley and cover with water.

2. Bring to a boil then reduce heat; simmer for 25 minutes.

3. Remove potatoes and parsley from water and mash using a potato masher or fork. Add water as needed if mixture is too dense.

4. Add sour cream. With a fork or whisk, combine into a smooth mix with no lumps. Refrigerate for 5 days or freeze in an airtight container for up to 6 months.

Cream Cheese Icing R

You can use this yummy icing as the final touch on lots of doggie goodies. Not only is it delicious, the yogurt has health benefits for canines, too. Along with animal protein, yogurt offers calcium, vitamins B_2 and B_{12}, potassium, and magnesium.

YIELDS: 1 cup

8 ounces cream cheese, softened

2 tablespoons low-fat plain yogurt

2–3 tablespoons all-purpose flour

1. Combine cream cheese and yogurt in a medium bowl, stirring to mix. Slowly add in flour a bit at a time until desired consistency is reached.

2. Refrigerate icing and treats after decorating. Refrigerate for 5 days or freeze in an airtight container for up to 6 months.

Bowser's Birthday Cupcake

Celebrate your dog's birthday or gotcha day with this cupcake that's pretty enough for photos. Liver icing makes it a canine favorite. Our 65-pound dogs enjoyed an entire cupcake each, but smaller dogs will need to have only a portion of the cupcake and save some of the birthday fun for the next day's treat.

YIELDS: 4 large cupcakes

Cupcakes:

1 cup white flour

1 egg

¼ cup organic unsweetened peanut butter

¼ cup Pumpkin Purée (see Chapter 15)

1 teaspoon baking soda

4 tablespoons (¼ cup) butter, melted

½ cup water

Frosting:

¼ pound chicken liver, rinsed and cooked

4 ounces cream cheese, warmed nearly to room temperature

1. Preheat oven to 350°F. Spray or grease a large cupcake tin.

2. In a large bowl, combine all cupcake ingredients, mixing thoroughly.

3. Divide mixture into four large cupcake tins. Bake until a toothpick inserted in the center of a cupcake comes out clean, approximately 30 minutes.

4. Set aside to cool completely on a wire rack before frosting.

5. To prepare the frosting: In a medium bowl, add the chicken liver. Use a fork to mash the chicken liver to a fine consistency. Add cream cheese and mix thoroughly using a fork or a hand mixer. Refrigerate any leftovers for 3 days or freeze in an airtight container for up to 6 months.

CHAPTER 11

International Fare

Would you and your pooch like a quick trip to the Caribbean? Or how about an evening in jolly old England? It's an easy order with one of our international doggie dishes, ones that you can share with your dog for a taste of travel in your own home. Though they don't typically like spicy food, dogs can appreciate different flavors now and then. The tastes in these dishes are unique, but the ingredients are still easy to find and are loved by all types of dogs.

Anise Seed Dog Treats

Anise is an herb that has been prized for centuries for its aromatic properties, and some dogs react to anise like cats to catnip. Used to impart a sweet taste in licorice, the seeds also make flavorful dog treats.

YIELDS: 20 (1½") treats

2 cups all-purpose flour

4 tablespoons (¼ cup) butter, softened to room temperature

¼ cup molasses

1 egg

2 teaspoons anise seed

1 teaspoon baking powder

1. Preheat oven to 350°F. Grease two cookie sheets.

2. Mix all the ingredients together in a large bowl; the result is a heavy, slightly sticky dough.

3. Pinch small pieces about the size of a large marble, roll between your palms, and slightly flatten with a fork before placing on the cookie sheets.

4. Bake; these cook quickly, so they'll be ready in about 15 minutes.

5. Let them cool completely before refrigerating (and your kitchen will smell wonderful in the meantime!). Refrigerate for 5 days or freeze in an airtight container for up to 6 months.

················· **Anise Adds Extra Fun** ·················

Anise seeds can also be used to create scented dog toys, much like catnip toys for felines. A spoonful of anise seeds can be sewn inside one of your dog's plush toys. Not all dogs react to the spice (just as not all cats react to catnip!), but those that do find the scent delightful!

Shepherd's Favorite Pie GF

Also known as cottage pie, this easy-to-prepare casserole can be a favorite with Shepherds—not to mention Collies, Boxers, and every other breed.

YIELDS: 9 cups

1 large potato

2 medium sweet potatoes

1 pound chicken (any cut), cooked

½ pound chicken heart, cooked

¼ cup chicken broth

2 tablespoons bacon fat, melted (optional)

1 cup shredded carrots

2 stalks celery, minced

1 cup low-fat cottage cheese

1. Preheat oven to 350°F.

2. Peel and quarter the potatoes, making sure to remove any green parts, then boil them until both types are tender.

3. Finely chop chicken and chicken hearts, removing any fat; mix with chicken broth and bacon fat (if using) in a large bowl. Add carrots and celery, then place in a 9" × 13" baking dish. Top with cottage cheese.

4. Mash potatoes; you can mix the types of potatoes together or keep them separate to create white and orange rows.

5. Spread potatoes on top of casserole, either spreading with a fork or piping them onto the casserole. If spreading, use a fork to create peaks in the potatoes for browning.

6. Bake for 40 minutes. Cool before serving. Refrigerate for 3 days or freeze in an airtight container for up to 6 months.

Caribbean Canine Coolers GF R

This recipe is a great use for bananas that are getting a little mushy . . . the dogs won't mind!

YIELDS: 3 cups, or 42 ice cubes

3 cups plain yogurt

1 cup shredded, unsweetened coconut flakes

1 tablespoon blackstrap molasses

1 large mango, peeled

2 bananas, peeled

1. Toss all of your ingredients in a blender and blend for 1–2 minutes until smooth.

2. Pour mixture into ice cube trays or small plastic tubs and freeze for a cool island treat for you or your dog!

······· **Most Fruits Are Cool for Canines** ·······

You can always substitute other fruits (just *never* grapes or raisins!) and you can leave out the unsweetened coconut flakes if you don't have any on hand.

Fido's Flautas

Black beans are a canine superfood. Their role in regulating a dog's blood sugar can help prevent diabetes. Black beans contain resistant starch that acts like fiber to reduce blood sugar as well as help with weight management for your dog—and they're even packed with antioxidants!

YIELDS: 9 flautas

2 cooked, deboned chicken breasts

1 cup cooked black beans, drained (canned are fine)

9 whole-wheat flour tortillas

½ cup shredded Cheddar or Monterey jack cheese

1. Preheat oven to 350°F. Lightly grease a cookie sheet.

2. Shred chicken using two forks. Use a fork to mash black beans.

3. Spread each tortilla with a thin coat of black beans, then add shredded chicken and cheese. Roll tightly. Secure with a toothpick.

4. Place flautas on cookie sheet, seam side down, and bake for 20 minutes until tortillas are golden brown and crispy.

5. Remove toothpicks and cool completely before serving. Refrigerate for 3 days or freeze in an airtight container for up to 6 months.

Pollution Solution

To help reduce gas emissions from your dog, soak dried beans overnight to rid the beans of raffinose, the sugar complex that causes much of the gas. Pour off the water, add new water, and bring to a boil. Skim off the foam and discard, adding more water as needed.

South Pacific Hot Dogs GF

Pineapple is a good source of calcium and potassium for your pooch. You can prepare these nuggets with all-beef, turkey, or organic hot dogs.

YIELDS: 100 treats

1 package (10) all-beef hot dogs

½ pineapple, peeled, cored, diced, and drained

1. Preheat oven to 350°F. Line a cookie sheet with parchment paper.

2. Slice each hot dog into 10 pieces. Place hot dog slices on cookie sheet and top with pineapple. Bake for 20 minutes.

3. Cool completely before serving. Refrigerate for 3 days or freeze in an airtight container for up to 6 months.

Once Really Is Enough!

If your dog suffers from coprophagia—eating his own or other dogs' feces—pineapple can be a good solution. Although most dogs like to eat pineapple, it is not appealing to the dog the second time around, and it can help break this difficult habit.

Pumpkin Rice

We first discovered pumpkin rice when traveling in Jamaica. This canine-friendly version omits the traditional spices and the Scotch Bonnet peppers.

YIELDS: 9 cups

1 tablespoon extra-virgin olive oil

2 cups frozen mixed vegetables (without onions)

1 cup Pumpkin Purée (see Chapter 15)

2 cups chicken or vegetable broth

2 cups uncooked instant brown rice

1. In a large saucepan, heat oil over medium heat. Add vegetables, Pumpkin Purée, and broth, bringing to a boil. Stir occasionally.

2. When mixture boils, stir in rice and again bring to a boil. Reduce heat to low and cook for 5 minutes.

3. Remove from heat and allow mixture to stand for 10 minutes or until all liquid is absorbed by the rice and vegetables. Fluff with a fork.

4. Allow dish to cool completely before serving to your dog. Refrigerate for 3–4 days or freeze in an airtight container for up to 6 months.

Sharing Meals

Sharing meals and treats with your dog is fun, not just for international fare, but also for many of the dog dishes in this cookbook. You'll find that only two aspects of your portion and your dog's portion differ: the amount of spice and the temperature at which the dish is served. The recipes in this cookbook are nonspicy, definitely preferred by dogs, and both meals and treats are intended to be served only slightly warm. You might find that you want your version a little spicier and served warmer.

Scottie's Scotch Eggs

Here's a traditional British favorite that you can share with your pooch.

YIELDS: 4 eggs

1 pound mild ground pork sausage (without onions)

¾ cup panko bread crumbs

2 tablespoons all-purpose flour

1 egg, beaten

4 hard-boiled eggs

1. Preheat oven to 400°F.

2. Shape sausage into four patties. Pour bread crumbs into a small bowl. Pour flour into a separate small bowl. Pour beaten egg into a third small bowl.

3. Roll each hard-boiled egg in flour to coat. Place egg on a sausage patty and shape the sausage around the egg.

4. Dip the sausage-covered egg into the beaten egg, then roll in the bread crumbs until entirely coated.

5. Place coated sausage-egg on cookie sheet and bake for 30–40 minutes until sausage is entirely cooked.

6. Cool before serving to canines. Refrigerate for 3–4 days.

Spaghetti Squash Primavera GF P

This grain-free dish can be shared with your four-legged family members.

YIELDS: 3 cups

1 teaspoon olive oil

¼ cup diced zucchini

¼ cup diced green bell pepper

¼ cup diced carrots

1 clove garlic, minced

1 plum tomato, diced

1 tablespoon water

2 cups cooked spaghetti squash

¼ cup grated Parmesan cheese

1. Heat oil over low heat in a medium skillet. Add zucchini, bell pepper, carrots, and garlic, cooking until tender. Stir to prevent sticking.

2. Add tomato and water; cook an additional 5 minutes.

3. Serve over spaghetti squash, topping with cheese.

4. Cool to room temperature before serving dog's portion. Refrigerate for 5 days or freeze in an airtight container for up to 6 months.

CHAPTER 12

Meaty Meals

Would you like to prepare a special dish for your dog for Sunday dinner? These meaty meals—including many fishy meals—appeal to your little carnivore with tasty ingredients ranging from lamb to sardines and beef to salmon. We've included a wide variety of recipes: traditional, raw, Paleo, and grain-free. As we mentioned in the introduction to this book, if you choose to go an entirely homemade route with your dog, you'll want to speak with your veterinarian for information on supplements, including calcium supplementation, an important element if your dog is not being fed digestible bones.

Slow-Cooked Canine Chicken

Using a slow cooker is a great time saver; it's essentially a set-it-and-forget-it proposition. While you are sleeping, your cooker gradually melds the ingredients into a delicious meal. In the morning, your kitchen will smell amazing!

YIELDS: About 9 cups

1 cup uncooked brown rice

3 boneless, skinless chicken breasts

2 carrots, cut into 1" rounds

1 sweet potato, cubed (unpeeled but with any green parts removed)

½ cup cranberries

Water, as needed

1. Add all ingredients to a 4-quart (or larger) slow cooker and cover with water.

2. Cook on low overnight, about 12 hours.

3. Cool before serving or refrigerating. Refrigerate for 3 days or freeze in an airtight container for up to 6 months.

Crockology 101

Make sure your slow cooker can fit these ingredients; it should only be about ¾ full when you begin cooking. The low setting on most cookers is about 200°F.

Raw Chicken Dinner ®

You can serve this chicken dinner boneless, with finely ground bones, or with whole bones, depending on your dog's eating habits and your comfort feeding your dog digestible bones. Many raw feeders feed edible bones—chicken wings and necks—either by giving them to the dog as part of the meal or grinding them first. Bones include important nutrients that otherwise must be provided in supplements.

YIELDS: 3 cups

1 pound raw chicken, chopped

2 whole chicken livers, rinsed and chopped

1 egg

½ clove garlic, chopped (optional)

2 tablespoons low-fat plain yogurt

1 teaspoon raw honey

1 tablespoon organic apple cider vinegar

½ teaspoon flaxseed oil

1 teaspoon kelp seaweed powder

1 teaspoon alfalfa powder

1. Mix all ingredients in a large bowl with a spoon, then portion meal based on your dog's size.

2. Refrigerate for 3 days or freeze in an airtight container for up to 6 months.

Powerful Powders

Kelp powder is a popular nutritional supplement for pets and adds a savory touch to pet recipes. Kelp is a good source of iron, potassium, calcium, manganese, and vitamins B_6, C, and K, as well as dietary fiber. Another component of this seaweed is glutamic acid, credited as being a natural food tenderizer. Alfalfa ("father of foods" in Arabic) was a valued food source for Arabian horses and is still recognized for its fiber, protein, and thirteen different vitamins. It also has antioxidant and antifungal properties.

Salmon Balls

Salmon is a great source of omega-3 fatty acids, so get ready to see a shiny coat when you add salmon to your dog's diet!

YIELDS: 12 (2") balls

1½ cups cooked salmon, chopped

1 cup cooked brown rice

1 egg

1 tablespoon olive oil

1. Preheat oven to 350°F. Lightly grease a cookie sheet or line with parchment paper.

2. In a medium bowl, combine all ingredients thoroughly. Use a spoon or melon baller to scoop mixture and roll into 12 balls. Place on cookie sheet.

3. Bake for 15 minutes. Allow treats to cool before serving or refrigerating. Refrigerate for 3–4 days or freeze in an airtight container for up to 6 months.

Sardine Cakes

Because they are high in omega-3 and -6 fatty acids, sardines are a superfood according to some people. Your dog will just think they're very tasty!

YIELDS: 6–9 (3") cakes (depending on the size of the sweet potatoes)

2 cooked sweet potatoes

2 (3.75-ounce) cans sardines in water, drained and chopped

1 clove garlic, crushed (optional)

1 egg, beaten

2 tablespoons all-purpose flour

1½ cups panko bread crumbs, divided

Olive oil, as needed

1. Peel sweet potato skins and mash potatoes in a large bowl. Add sardines, garlic (if using), egg, and flour; mix thoroughly. Stir in 1 cup of bread crumbs and mix completely.

2. Shape mixture into small 3" patties. Roll patties in remaining bread crumbs.

3. In a large skillet, heat about 2 tablespoons of olive oil over medium-high heat. Fry two or three sardine patties at a time for about 5–8 minutes, flipping halfway, until golden brown.

4. Drain on a paper towel and cool completely before serving to your dog. Cool before serving or refrigerating. Refrigerate for 3–4 days or freeze in an airtight container for up to six months.

Beef Fried Rice

You and your dog can share this recipe; add a little hot pepper sauce to your portion, leaving your dog's portion a bit blander.

YIELDS: 6–7 cups

2 cups water

1 cup uncooked jasmine rice

2 eggs

1 pound lean ground beef

½ cup sliced celery

½ cup low-sodium soy sauce

1 tablespoon sesame oil

½ cup frozen chopped carrots and peas

1. In a medium saucepan, bring water to a boil over high heat. Once boiling, add the rice and stir. Return the pot to a boil, then lower heat to low, cover, and simmer the rice until tender and all the water is absorbed, about 18–25 minutes. Fluff with a fork and set aside.

2. Spray large skillet with nonstick cooking spray and heat over medium heat.

3. Beat eggs in a small bowl, then pour into skillet and cook until firm.

4. Remove from heat and slice eggs into strips. Combine eggs with rice and set aside; return skillet to stove.

5. Spray skillet again if needed. Cook ground beef and celery over medium heat until beef is thoroughly cooked (about 10 minutes), stirring to prevent sticking and overbrowning.

6. In a small bowl, combine soy sauce and sesame oil, then pour over beef mixture. Add carrots and peas, cooked rice, and cooked egg strips, stirring constantly for 3–4 minutes to thoroughly combine and warm ingredients.

7. Cool dog's portion before serving. Refrigerate for 3–4 days or freeze in an airtight container for up to 3 months.

Lots of Other Options

This dish is easily customizable. Sliced almonds, chopped peanuts, chopped broccoli, cooked chicken, pea pods, and bamboo shoots make other tasty additions for this dish for you and your dog.

Terrier's Tuna Casserole

**Tuna makes a tasty meal to share with your dog;
you might want to add mayonnaise to your portion.**

YIELDS: 2 cups

1 (9-ounce) can tuna packed in
water

1 cup cooked pasta, drained

½ cup frozen peas, thawed

¼ cup chopped fresh parsley

¼ cup grated Parmesan cheese

1. Drain tuna, reserving the tuna water to use in place of water in a treat recipe.

2. In a medium bowl, mix tuna, pasta, peas, parsley, and cheese. Serve.

3. Refrigerate unused portions. Refrigerate for 3 days or freeze in an airtight container for up to 3 months.

Chicken and Rice Tender Tummy Meal

This easy-to-make meal is recommended for dogs with an upset stomach. Like mom's chicken soup, this meal is easy on the tummy. Start with a small serving, perhaps just spoonfuls, until your dog's appetite returns.

YIELDS: 6 cups

2 chicken breasts

2 quarts water

1 cup white rice

1. Remove and discard bones, fat, and skin from chicken breasts.

2. In a soup pot, bring the water to a boil. Add chicken breasts and cook thoroughly until there is no pink showing in the meat.

3. When chicken is done, remove it from the water; add rice to the water and reduce heat to medium. Cook until rice is tender and slightly overdone (at least 30 minutes). Remove from burner while it cools and absorbs additional water. After 30 minutes, pour off additional water but leave moist and slightly soupy.

4. While the rice is cooking, shred the chicken using two forks.

5. When the rice is cooked, return chicken to pot and cool completely before serving. Refrigerate for 3 days or freeze in an airtight container for up to 6 months.

White or Brown Rice?

White rice is always recommended over brown rice for dogs with an upset tummy. (Brown rice contains more fiber.) Chicken breast is also preferred over other cuts of meats, since it contains less fat and grease.

Stuffed Pumpkin ⓖⓕ

This multimeal one-dish creation combines some of the healthiest fall foods for Fido in one easy-to-prepare creation.

YIELDS: 10 cups

1 (3-pound) cooking pumpkin

1 apple

1 cup green beans, cooked

½ pound ground turkey or ground chicken

2 tablespoons grated Parmesan cheese

1. Preheat oven to 350°F.

2. Remove top of pumpkin; using a spoon, remove all seeds from the pumpkin. (Set seeds aside for a future recipe.)

3. Core apple; discard the core and seeds and finely chop. Chop green beans.

4. In a medium bowl, mix green beans, apple, turkey, and Parmesan cheese. Stuff into pumpkin cavity. Place pumpkin on a baking sheet on the middle rack and bake for 1 hour.

5. Drain any accumulating liquid from the top of the pumpkin during cooking.

6. Cool completely before serving. To serve, cut pumpkin in half. Scoop meal, including pumpkin flesh, from the pumpkin. Refrigerate unused portions for up to 3 days or freeze in an airtight container for up to 2 months.

Salmon and Spinach Hash GF

We love the ease of one-dish meals both for our dogs and ourselves. This meal may be simple, but it packs a big nutritional punch!

YIELDS: 4 cups

1 teaspoon olive oil

1 (7.5-ounce) can salmon, drained

1 cup frozen spinach, thawed

4 eggs

1. Heat olive oil in a medium skillet over medium-high heat. Add salmon and spinach, stirring until completely heated.

2. Add eggs and scramble.

3. Cool before serving. Refrigerate for up to 3 days.

Lamb Hash

Lamb is one of those ingredients that really perks up our dogs' ears. (Yes, they know the word "lamb"!) This dish is easy to prepare and freezes well for later meals. Larger neighborhood groceries carry ground lamb regularly, and it's a staple at many specialty groceries and at most organic food markets.

YIELDS: 7 cups

2 tablespoons olive oil

1 pound ground lamb

1 cup frozen mixed vegetables (without onions)

2 cups cooked brown rice

2 cups cooked white rice

1 cup low-fat plain yogurt

1. In a large skillet, heat olive oil over medium-high heat. Cook lamb until no longer pink, about 10 minutes, and drain off fat.

2. Add vegetables, stirring to defrost. Remove from heat.

3. In a large bowl, combine lamb mixture, rice, and yogurt. Mix thoroughly.

4. Cool before serving.

5. Refrigerate for 3 days or freeze in an airtight container for up to 6 months.

Buffalo Meatballs

It's always interesting to see how dogs respond to new taste sensations. When we first served bison meat instead of their regular beef, Irie and Tiki didn't hesitate. They loved it!

YIELDS: About 30 (1") meatballs

2 slices whole-wheat bread, cut into ½" cubes

½ cup milk

1 egg

⅓ cup grated Parmesan cheese

2 tablespoons finely chopped parsley

1 pound ground bison

Olive oil, for frying

1. In a medium bowl, soak bread cubes in milk until soft (about 5 minutes). Remove bread from milk, squeeze out extra milk, and discard milk.

2. In a large bowl, combine bread, egg, cheese, parsley, and bison. Pinch off small pieces and roll into balls.

3. In a large skillet, heat ½ cup olive oil over medium-high heat. Fry each meatball until no longer pink in the center, approximately 8–10 minutes.

4. Remove from heat to cool completely before serving. Refrigerate for 3–4 days or freeze in an airtight container for up to 6 months.

Trim That Fat

Compared to many other meats, bison is a low-fat choice. One hundred grams (3½ ounces) of bison has only 2.42 grams of fat, compared to 8–10 grams for beef, nearly 10 for pork, over 7 for chicken, and more than 10 for sockeye salmon.

Turkey Kibble

Although kibble isn't the first choice in most homemade diets, this is still a good recipe to have on hand. Kibble works well if you're traveling and need to bring along some meals for your dog.

YIELDS: About 2 pounds of kibble

8½ cups whole-wheat flour

2 cups nonfat dry milk powder

2 eggs

½ cup extra-virgin olive oil

1 pound uncooked lean ground turkey

2 cups puréed, cooked sweet potato without skin (or substitute pumpkin, green beans, or a mix)

1. Preheat oven to 200°F. Lightly oil a cookie sheet and set aside.

2. In a large bowl, mix flour, dry milk powder, eggs, and olive oil. Add ground turkey and vegetable purée. Mix well.

3. Roll dough on a lightly floured surface to ¼"–½" thickness. Transfer dough to cookie sheet.

4. Score dough with a pizza cutter to create size-appropriate kibble pieces.

5. Bake for 90 minutes. Turn off oven and allow kibble to cool and harden.

6. When cool, remove from oven and break along score lines into kibble. Bag and refrigerate for up to 3 days.

Traveling with Toto

Planning a trip with your dog but want to keep feeding him a homemade diet? Besides taking your own food, it's easy to order food for your dog at restaurants along your way as well. Grilled chicken breasts and hamburger patties are universal. Pair the meat with Lentil Loaves (see Chapter 14) from home and your dog will be set!

Chicken and Sardine Kibble

Making your own kibble not only gives you total control over your dog's diet, it can also be an economical alternative to pricey commercial kibble. You can buy chicken gizzards in the poultry section of the grocery store . . . and they're cheap!

YIELDS: About 2 pounds of kibble

3 sweet potatoes, baked

1½ cups water, divided

1 pound cooked chicken gizzards

1 (3.75-ounce) can sardines in water

9½ cups whole-wheat flour

2 cups nonfat dry milk powder

3 eggs

¾ cup extra-virgin olive oil

1. Preheat oven to 250°F. Lightly oil two cookie sheets.

2. Peel sweet potatoes; discard peels. Purée sweet potatoes with ¾ cup water in a blender or food processor. (This makes about 2½ cups.) Set aside.

3. Finely chop gizzards with ¾ cups water in a blender or food processor. Add sardines and blend until smooth.

4. In a large bowl, mix flour, milk powder, eggs, and olive oil. Add sweet potato purée and chopped gizzards and sardines. Mix well.

5. Turn out dough on a floured surface. (The dough will be thick and sticky.) Add more flour as needed. Work dough to an even consistency, then roll out dough to ¼"–½" thick.

6. Cut strips with a pizza cutter and place on cookie sheets. Strips should be at least ½" apart on the cookie sheets.

7 Bake for 45 minutes, then turn strips. Use pizza cutter to cut strips into ½" squares (or smaller, depending on dog's size). Return cookie sheets to the oven and bake for 45 more minutes.

8 Turn off the oven. Use a spatula to flip all squares and make sure squares aren't touching. Return cookie sheet to the oven and leave to cool, or if you have another batch that needs to cook, move kibble to drying racks to cool.

9 When kibble is cool, store 1 week's worth in refrigerator and freeze the remaining kibble in an airtight container for up to 6 months.

Substituting Flour

If your dog has wheat allergies, it's easy to swap out rice, buckwheat, quinoa, nut, and oat flour in your recipes. The gluten found in wheat flour gives baked goods their springy feel, so to compensate, you'll need to add a thickening agent like guar gum (which is also used in many wet, commercial dog foods).

Buffalo Hash

Buffalo has a lower fat content than beef and about half the cholesterol. If you don't have ground buffalo on hand, though, you can substitute ground beef, chicken, or turkey in this easy recipe.

YIELDS: 7 cups

2 tablespoons olive oil

1 pound ground buffalo

2 eggs

2 cups frozen chopped vegetables (without onion)

2 cups cooked brown rice

1. In a large skillet, heat olive oil over medium-high heat. Add ground buffalo, stirring and cooking until buffalo is no longer pink, about 10 minutes.

2. Drain off any excess fat, then add in eggs, chopped vegetables, and brown rice, reducing heat to medium. Continue stirring and cook until eggs are cooked. Cool before serving or refrigerating. Refrigerate for up to 3 days or freeze in an airtight container for 6 months.

Buffalo Is Lean and Clean

For many diners, buffalo is a big draw because typically, buffalo do not require the antibiotics that beef cattle do. They are raised without growth hormones as well. Buffalo pretty much go to pasture and do their own thing!

Chicken Meatloaf

Meatloaf is the very definition of comfort food, and it's a favorite with many pet parents who feed a homemade diet. Meatloaves are easy to prepare and freeze; you can even double or triple the recipe to cook in bulk.

YIELDS: 8 cups

½ cup barley

4 cups Homemade Chicken Broth (see Chapter 15)

1½ pounds ground chicken

½ cup low-fat cottage cheese

2 whole eggs

½ cup rolled oats

¾ cup finely chopped carrots

1 tablespoon olive oil

1. In a medium saucepan, bring barley and chicken broth to a boil, then reduce heat to simmer for 45 minutes. Set aside to cool.

2. Preheat oven to 350°F. Lightly spray a 9" × 13" baking dish.

3. In a large bowl, mix ground chicken, cottage cheese, eggs, rolled oats, carrots, and olive oil. Mix well. Slowly add cooled barley and broth. Mix thoroughly.

4. Place mixture in pan and bake for 1 hour.

5. Cool before serving. Refrigerate for 3 days or freeze in an airtight container for up to 6 months.

Veggie Substitutes

Change up this meatloaf by substituting other vegetables in place of the carrots: Try peas, zucchini, broccoli, asparagus, spinach, or your dog's other favorites.

Eggshell Calcium GF R P

Unless your homemade diet includes raw meaty bones, you'll need to add a calcium supplement. Eggshell calcium is a great way to use those shells you'd otherwise discard.

YIELDS: About 12 teaspoons

12 eggshells

1. Collect washed eggshells in the refrigerator until you have 1 dozen or enough to fill a cookie sheet. Eggshells will begin to dry while in the refrigerator.

2. Preheat oven to 200°F.

3. Spread the eggshells on a cookie sheet and bake for 10–15 minutes. They should be completely dry. (If you washed the eggshells shortly before baking, allow extra baking time. Eggshells must be completely dry before grinding.)

4. Grind the eggshells in a clean coffee grinder or a blender until all large pieces are ground to a powder. A mortar and pestle is also a great way to grind to a powder.

5. Store in a lidded jar. Store in a dry place for up to 2 months.

Egg-cellent Calcium

If you're feeding a homemade diet, you'll want to add about ½ teaspoon ground eggshell per pound of fresh food. If you feed both fresh food and commercial food, just add the eggshell to the fresh portion of the meal.

Mutt Meatloaf Meal ⓖⓕ

Quick and easy to prepare, this whole meal can be made ahead of time to offer several days of breakfasts and dinners for your dog.

YIELDS: 16 cups

4 pounds lean ground turkey

½ pound organic beef liver or chicken liver, rinsed and diced

4 eggs

2 cups puréed carrots, steamed

2 cups puréed potatoes, steamed

2 cups puréed green beans, steamed

1. Preheat oven to 350°F.

2. Combine all ingredients and divide into four 8" × 4" × 2½" loaf pans. Each should be about ¾ full. Bake for 1 hour. Drain off any grease.

3. Cool and refrigerate 1 week's worth of food. Double-wrap remaining meatloaf in foil or place in a zip-top plastic bag and freeze for up to 6 months.

More Meatloaf Options

Ground chicken, ground lamb, or ground beef can be substituted in this recipe. Other substitutions include broccoli (with stems), asparagus, sweet potatoes, cauliflower, peas, squash, zucchini, and more.

Raw Meatloaf GF R

This template for an easy-to-prepare raw loaf can serve as the framework for the meat and vegetables that are on sale at your local market. An excellent way to take advantage of seasonal produce, the meatloaf provides enough variety for your dog to never grow bored of his meals.

YIELDS: 6 cups

1 pound raw ground beef, bison, lamb, turkey, or chicken

2 cups puréed vegetables

¼ cup liver, gizzards, or kidneys, rinsed

½ cup organic apple cider vinegar

½ cup low-fat plain yogurt

3 eggs with shells, finely broken

Mix all ingredients together in a large bowl. Refrigerate for 3 days or freeze in an airtight container for up to 6 months.

······· **Raw Power** ·······

Australian veterinarian Dr. Ian Billinghurst, author of *Give Your Dog a Bone*, is the founder of the BARF, or Biologically Appropriate Raw Food, movement. Designed using raw meat, finely ground bones, offal, fruits, and vegetables, the BARF diet mimics the evolutionary diet of dogs.

Spot's Spinach and Sprats

Popeye's favorite muscle food is also beneficial for dogs when fed in moderate quantities. Spinach is full of vitamins and is a good source of lutein, which promotes ocular health.

YIELDS: 6 cups

2 jumbo eggs

2 tablespoons olive oil

2 cups cooked brown rice, chilled

2 loose cups fresh spinach, chopped

1 (8.5-ounce) can sprats, drained and chopped

1. Spray a large skillet with nonstick spray. Break eggs into a small bowl and whip with a fork. Pour eggs into skillet and cook over medium heat until firm. Remove from heat.

2. Remove eggs from skillet and cut into strips.

3. Return skillet to stove over medium heat and add olive oil. Add rice to skillet, stirring continuously until warmed, then add spinach. Cook until spinach wilts. Add sprats and eggs, stirring until mixed.

4. Cool before serving. Refrigerate for 3 days or freeze in an airtight container for up to 6 months.

Sounds Fishy to Me

We've all heard of Jack Sprat, but what, exactly, are sprats? These tiny fish resemble sardines and sometimes pass for their maritime cousins in the grocery store. Like sardines, canned sprats are oily and fragrant, sure to appeal to the dog palate. They are a high-protein fish and are considered to be a good source of vitamin B_{12}.

CHAPTER 13

Breakfast Dishes

Our dogs like to get up early and head outside to patrol the yard before returning indoors for their breakfast. Of course, that means we are up early, too. It's nice that most of these doggie breakfasts can be prepared ahead of time and served in a jiffy. In fact, we sometimes use the same plan for our own breakfasts by making breakfast quiches that can be quickly reheated. Start your dog's day with healthy choices—and a great bonding experience—by cooking for the two of you!

Mini Liver Quiche GF

**Chicken liver and eggs
make an inexpensive base for this meal.**

YIELDS: 6 muffins

¼ pound chicken livers, rinsed and cooked

3 eggs

¼ cup diced, cooked green beans

1. Preheat oven to 350°F. Grease muffin tins or line with parchment cups.

2. Use the back of a fork to mash chicken livers, chopping any larger bits. Whisk eggs in a medium bowl, then fold in chicken livers and green beans.

3. Fill muffin tins with mixture ¾ full, then bake until golden brown, about 30 minutes, depending on the size of the muffins.

4. Cool completely before serving; refrigerate leftovers for up to 3 days.

Baked Egg Cups GF

These cute, protein-rich little goodies make a great way to start Rover's morning, although they will be welcome any time of day.

YIELDS: 16 mini-muffins

8 eggs

½ cup cottage cheese

½ teaspoon baking powder

1 cup shredded Cheddar cheese

½ cup shredded cooked chicken

1 (5-ounce) can tuna in water, drained

1 Preheat oven to 350°F. Line mini-muffin tin with parchment cups.

2 Whisk eggs in a large bowl, then add cottage cheese, baking powder, cheese, chicken, and tuna.

3 Fill each cup ⅔ full with egg mixture. Bake for 30 minutes.

4 Cool before serving. Refrigerate; egg cups last about 3 days.

Chia Seed Oatmeal ®

Want to make a nutritious breakfast for you and your dog to share? Prepare this dish at night and refrigerate overnight. You'll wake up to a yummy dish that uses chia, a superfood packed with omega-3 fatty acids, calcium, and more.

YIELDS: 4 cups

1 cup unsweetened almond milk

1 cup old-fashioned oats

2 tablespoons chia seeds

2 apples

2 tablespoons raw honey

1 teaspoon lemon juice

1 cup low-fat plain Greek yogurt

1. In a medium bowl, pour almond milk over oats and chia seeds. Set aside.

2. Peel, core, and grate the apples, tossing with honey and lemon juice. (Be sure to discard apple seeds.) Add apples and yogurt to chia seed and oats mixture.

3. Stir to mix well, cover, and refrigerate overnight. Chill at least 12 hours so the chia seeds will plump up. Refrigerate for up to 5 days.

Wake Up to Chia

Chia seeds date back to the Aztecs and Mayans but came to everyone's attention with Chia Pets, terracotta figurines that rose to popularity in the 1980s due to their sprouting chia "foliage" and "fur." Today, chia seeds are lauded for their nutritional properties, including the fact that they are a superior antioxidant, more than any other whole food.

Spinach Omelet GF P

Who doesn't like to start the day with an omelet? This simple recipe adds spinach for color and added nutrition.

YIELDS: 1 omelet

2 eggs

1 cup baby spinach leaves, torn

1 tablespoon grated Parmesan cheese

1. In a small bowl, beat the eggs, then add spinach and cheese. Pour into a nonstick skillet coated with cooking spray.

2. Cook over medium heat until partially set, about 5 minutes, then flip with spatula to cook to desired doneness.

3. Cool before serving. Refrigerate unused portion up to 3 days.

Cottage Cheese Breakfast GF R

This easy breakfast can be served to your dog—or you can start your day off right by making a portion for yourself, too!

YIELDS: 1 cup

⅓ cup cottage cheese

⅓ cup plain yogurt

⅓ cup mashed blueberries

Mix all ingredients together in a medium bowl and serve. If you have a small dog and only need a portion of this dish, you can store the remainder in the refrigerator for up to 5 days.

················ **More Yummy Choices** ················

Along with blueberries, other good options for this easy breakfast include puréed or finely chopped apple (discarding the core and seeds), puréed carrots, bananas, mashed blackberries, and other favorite fruits and vegetables your dog enjoys.

Fishermen's Eggs GF P

Ahoy, mateys! This seafood-inspired recipe will have all hands on deck at mess time, even for landlubber dogs.

YIELDS: 2 cups

1 (3.75-ounce) can sardines in water

2 tablespoons fresh parsley

4 eggs

1. Preheat oven to 375°F. Coat an oven-safe 8" × 8" casserole dish with nonstick spray.

2. Drain sardines (reserve water for another recipe or a tasty topping for your dog's food). Chop sardines and mix with parsley.

3. Line the prepared dish with the sardine mixture, then top with eggs. (Either beat the eggs and pour over the sardines or crack each egg individually on a different portion of the mixture.)

4. Bake until eggs are cooked to desired doneness, about 15 minutes.

5. Cool before serving to your dog. Refrigerate for 3 days or freeze in an airtight container for up to 6 months.

········· **Other Fish in the Sea** ················

Salmon or shrimp make tasty substitutions for this dish; you can also add your dog's favorite vegetables to the sardine layer. Carrots, sweet potato, green beans, pumpkin, celery, peas, and other vegetables can create different versions of this canine favorite.

Raw Breakfast

Start the day without cooking, thanks to this raw Bowser breakfast. This recipe makes a single meal for a 30- to 40-pound dog and can also be prepared in bulk and frozen.

YIELDS: 1 serving

1 egg

1 chicken liver, rinsed

1 ounce muscle meat or heart

½ teaspoon organic apple cider vinegar

2 tablespoons plain yogurt, cottage cheese, or kefir

1 teaspoon flaxseed oil

½ teaspoon raw honey

1 frozen Raw Veggie Cupcake, thawed (see Chapter 14)

1. Crack egg into a large bowl and break up eggshell into small pieces.

2. Add chicken liver and muscle meat; stir in apple cider vinegar, yogurt, flaxseed oil, and honey before serving.

3. Serve with Raw Veggie Cupcake for a full breakfast.

Honey: Sweet by Any Name

Most honey sold in stores has been pasteurized, but you can find raw honey in farmers' markets and specialty stores. Unpasteurized, unfiltered, and unclarified, this raw honey will be labeled "100 percent pure." Honey has long been praised as a great source of antioxidants and for its antimicrobial properties.

Deviled Eggs GF P

Deviled eggs are a family tradition at our get-togethers. This doggie version adds chicken livers for added taste and nutrition.

YIELDS: 12 half-eggs

6 eggs

Water, as needed

¼ cup rinsed and cooked puréed chicken livers

1 teaspoon organic apple cider vinegar

1. Place whole eggs in a single layer in a saucepan, cover with water, and heat until boiling. Cover the pot, reduce heat to low, and cook for 1 more minute.

2. Remove eggs from heat and leave covered for 15 minutes. Uncover and rinse eggs in cold water for 1 minute.

3. Crack and peel eggs under running water. Set eggs aside.

4. Slice eggs lengthwise and remove yolks, placing them in a medium bowl. Add chicken liver purée to bowl along with apple cider vinegar. Mash the yolks, chicken livers, and vinegar to a fine crumble.

5. Disperse the egg yolk mixture into the egg whites. These tasty eggs can be refrigerated 3 days (if they last that long!).

CHAPTER 14

Side Dishes

What's dinner without side dishes? While we've included many one-dish meals like meatloaf and hash that incorporate vegetables, it's also fun to cook up (or serve raw) a tasty side dish with a meaty meal. These sides also can be served as flavorful, nutritional treats by just serving treat-size portions and freezing the remainder. Sides also make a great way to prepare seasonal fruits and vegetables and add them to your dog's favorite meat dish.

Pepitas GF

Don't discard those pumpkin seeds! Seeds are filled with protein, amino acids, fiber, iron, copper, phosphorus, magnesium, calcium, zinc, potassium, folic acid, and niacin. Seeds can be ground and used in recipes or as a topping for food.

YIELDS: ½–2 cups, depending on pumpkin size

1 pumpkin

1 tablespoon extra-virgin olive oil

1. Scoop seeds from pumpkin. (Save pumpkin to use in one of the pumpkin recipes.)

2. Wash seeds in a large colander, discarding any pulp. Spread out seeds on a cookie sheet and allow to dry overnight.

3. Preheat oven to 250°F. Gather seeds in a zip-top plastic bag and add extra-virgin olive oil. Shake bag so all seeds are coated with oil.

4. Pour seeds onto the baking sheet. (You can season half the sheet for your own snacks and leave the other half plain for your dog.)

5. Bake 1 hour until golden brown. Cool before refrigerating.

A Natural Dewormer

Raw pepitas can be dried and ground in a clean coffee grinder to a powder. The seeds contain cucurbitin, a natural dewormer. Talk with your vet about using this powder on your dog's food, usually served as 1 teaspoon per 10 pounds of your dog's weight until signs of parasites are gone.

Kanine Kale and Kiwi GF P

Paired with your dog's favorite meat dish, this side dish is healthy and flavorful. The kiwi is also packed with fiber, potassium, and vitamin C, while kale is considered one of the healthiest vegetables around for both dogs and humans.

YIELDS: 3 cups

2 teaspoons coconut oil

1 clove garlic, chopped

1 teaspoon peeled and minced fresh ginger

1 tablespoon fresh oregano leaves

2 kiwis, peeled and chopped

1 bunch kale, washed and sliced into thin strips

1. In a large skillet, heat coconut oil over medium-high heat. Add garlic and ginger and heat for 3 minutes, stirring. Add oregano and kiwi, and continue stirring for another 2 minutes.

2. Reduce heat to low and add kale; cook about 5 minutes until kale is tender.

3. Remove from heat and cool before serving your dog.

4. Refrigerate leftovers for up to 5 days.

Kale Cautions

Despite its nutritional value, dogs with kidney disease or those prone to bladder infections should avoid this leafy green.

Lentil Loaves

Lentils make an excellent high-protein, low-calorie snack for dogs watching their waistlines.

YIELDS: 8 muffins

1 cup dry lentils

¼ cup shredded carrots

1 egg

1 cup old-fashioned oats

1. Preheat oven to 350°F. Grease a muffin tin or line with parchment cups.

2. Cook lentils according to package instructions until soft. Remove from heat and drain water. Pour lentils into a medium bowl.

3. Use a fork or a potato masher to mash lentils. Once cool, add carrots, egg, and oats; stir until completely mixed.

4. Pour mixture into muffin cups so they're ⅔ full.

5. Bake for 25 minutes.

6. Cool before serving. Refrigerate for 5 days or freeze in an airtight container for up to 6 months.

Kale Chips GF P

Although kale should be avoided by dogs with kidney disease or bladder stones, this green is great for dogs in need of a low-calorie but nutritionally rich treat.

YIELDS: 10–20 treat servings

1 head kale, washed and dried

2 tablespoons olive oil

1. Preheat oven to 275°F.

2. Remove ribs from kale and trim to 2" pieces. In a plastic bag, toss pieces with olive oil. Remove from bag and spread pieces on a cookie sheet.

3. Bake kale until crisp (about 20 minutes), turning leaves halfway.

········· **Nutrient-Rich Greens** ·········

Not only has kale been shown to prevent cancer and heart disease, it's also a great source of calcium; vitamins A, C, and E; and fiber. Although olive oil is healthier, if your dog doesn't enjoy the kale, try substituting 2 tablespoons of bacon fat.

Raw Veggie Cupcakes GF P R

Shop seasonally to take advantage of sales and freshness, substituting different greens as they become available.

YIELDS: 3–4 dozen mini cakes

1 head celery, trimmed

1 bundle carrots, trimmed

1 bunch parsley, trimmed

1 bunch kale, spinach greens, bok choy, mustard greens, or Romaine lettuce

1. Wash and trim all vegetables. (Other options include asparagus, broccoli, cauliflower, collards, cabbage, cucumbers, squash, sweet potatoes, and zucchini.)

2. Chop into squares and add to a food processor or blender, 1 cup at a time, to purée, adding water to mixture as needed.

3. Once all vegetables are puréed, combine all into one mix. Freeze in ice cube trays or in small cupcake holders.

4. To serve, remove from freezer and thaw to room temperature (or serve as a frozen treat).

············ **Unlocking Those Nutrients** ············

Puréeing vegetables breaks down the cellulose wall of the plants. Dogs can't digest cellulose, so puréeing makes the nutrients within the walls available to the dog.

Skinny Veggies GF

If your dog is eating a commercial diet but needs to lose weight, consider replacing a portion of the commercial food with cooked vegetables.

YIELDS: 4–5 cups

1 head broccoli, finely chopped

1 pound carrots, shredded

½ pound green beans, chopped

1. Mix vegetables together in a large bowl, cover, and store in refrigerator. To add to your dog's meal, portion out the meal's serving, add 1 tablespoon of water, and microwave for 3 minutes.

2. Cool before adding to food. Refrigerate for up to 5 days.

It's All Good!

When serving broccoli to your dog, don't worry about only using florets. Broccoli stalks are an excellent source of nutrition for your dog, and provide vitamins A and C, beta carotene, and calcium.

Sweet Potato Potstickers

You and your pooch can share these nutritional potstickers. Look for wonton wrappers in your grocery's refrigerated produce section or in the freezer section of Asian markets and supermarkets.

YIELDS: 12 potstickers

1 cup cooked sweet potato (roughly 2 medium sweet potatoes, peeled)

1 tablespoon fresh rosemary

⅓ cup ricotta cheese

¼ cup grated Parmesan cheese

12 wonton wrappers

1 tablespoon sunflower oil

1. Preheat oven to 350°F.

2. In a blender or food processor, combine sweet potato, rosemary, and cheeses and pulse until well blended.

3. Place 1 tablespoon of sweet potato and cheese mixture in the middle of a wonton wrapper; wet the edges of the wrapper with olive oil and crimp to close. Place the wonton on a baking sheet. Repeat until all wontons and filling are used.

4. Use a pastry brush to coat wontons with sunflower oil.

5. Bake for 15–20 minutes until golden brown.

6. Cool before serving to your dog or refrigerating. Refrigerate for 3 days or freeze in an airtight container for up to 6 months.

CHAPTER 15

Soups, Purées, and Gravies

The restorative power of soup and broth is something we have all experienced, whether it's Mom's homemade chicken soup when we're feeling sick, or as an appetizer before the main course of a meal. Dogs, too, love these tasty delights, and they are all easy to make and save for future use. This is also a good way to provide extra hydration to your pet. The gravies and toppers are very rich foods, so you won't want to feed more than a little bit at a time. Just a spoonful (or less for a tiny pooch) will pack a flavorful punch.

Homemade Chicken Broth GF P

Commercial chicken broth often contains onion, a no-no for dogs, and too much sodium. Homemade Chicken Broth is fast and easy to make and can be used in many recipes—even as a quick frozen treat.

YIELDS: 6–8 cups

1 (3-pound) chicken
Water, as needed

1. Place chicken in a large stockpot and cover with 3" of water.

2. Bring to a boil, then simmer for 1 hour.

3. Remove chicken from the water and reserve for another recipe. (Discard all cooked chicken bones because cooked bones are a splintering and choking hazard for dogs.)

4. Refrigerate broth until completely cooled. Skim off fat before freezing. Refrigerate for up to 3 days or freeze in an airtight container for up to 6 months.

············· **Frozen Favorites** ·············

Ice trays are a handy way to freeze Homemade Chicken Broth. Once frozen, store cubes in zip-top plastic bags for easy use in future treat recipes.

Pumpkin Purée GF P

Puréed pumpkin is an excellent addition to many dog treat and meal recipes. Canned pumpkin (never pumpkin pie filling) can also be used.

YIELDS: 2–4 cups

1 small cooking pumpkin

Water, as needed

1. Preheat oven to 350°F. Line a cookie sheet with parchment paper.

2. Wash pumpkin and cut off top. Divide pumpkin into quarters.

3. Use a spoon to remove seeds from each quarter, reserving seeds to later wash and dry for future recipes.

4. Place pumpkin quarters on baking sheet and bake for 30–40 minutes.

5. Remove from oven and cool. Remove baked pumpkin skin and discard.

6. Chop pumpkin into cubes; add cubes to a blender along with enough water to blend to the consistency of baby food.

7. Freeze purée in 1-cup containers or in ice cube trays. Once frozen, place cubes in a zip-top plastic bag or other airtight container and freeze for up to 6 months.

Easy on the Tummy

A tablespoon or two of Pumpkin Purée can help dogs with both constipation and diarrhea thanks to its fiber. Pumpkin is also a great food for plump dogs, as the fiber in it makes dogs feel fuller, even with diminished meal portions.

Chickpea Stew GF

You and your dog can share this nutrient-packed meal made with chickpeas (garbanzo beans), a canine superfood. It's excellent with a side dish of couscous.

YIELDS: 9 cups

- 1 tablespoon olive oil
- 1 cup (¼"-thick) carrot slices
- 1 teaspoon brown sugar
- 1 teaspoon peeled and grated fresh ginger
- 2 cloves garlic, minced
- 3 cups cooked chickpeas
- 1½ cups peeled and cubed baking potato
- 1 cup diced green bell pepper
- 1 cup (1") cut green beans
- 1 (14.5-ounce) can diced tomatoes, undrained
- 1¾ cups water or vegetable stock
- 3 cups fresh baby spinach
- 1 cup light coconut milk

1. In a large nonstick skillet, heat oil over medium heat. Add carrot and cook until tender, approximately 5 minutes. Stir in brown sugar, ginger, and garlic. Cook for 1 minute, stirring constantly to prevent sticking. Remove from heat.

2. Place mixture in a 5-quart slow cooker. Add chickpeas, potato, bell pepper, green beans, tomatoes, and water or stock. Cook on high for 6 hours or until vegetables are fork-tender.

3. Add spinach and coconut milk, stirring until spinach wilts. Cool before serving to dog. Refrigerate for up to 3 days.

Beneficial Beans

Like black beans and soybeans, chickpeas help regulate blood sugar in dogs. A source of natural fiber, the chickpeas also include many proteins and minerals that boost your dog's immune system.

Beef Stock GF P

Although you can easily purchase canned stock or bouillon cubes, many commercial stocks include onion. It's inexpensive and easy to make your own dog-friendly Beef Stock, which freezes well.

YIELDS: 2½ quarts

2 carrots, cut into 1" pieces

1 pound beef stew meat

5 pounds beef marrow bones

Olive oil, as needed

1 celery rib, cut into 1" pieces (or celery tops from several ribs)

2 cloves garlic

Water, as needed

···· **Cooked Bones Are a No-No** ····

Dogs should never chew cooked bones, which become brittle with cooking, so discard these out of your dog's reach!

1. Preheat oven to 400°F.

2. In a large roasting pan, spread out carrots, stew meat, and bones. Rub bones with olive oil to coat. Roast for 45 minutes, turning meat and bones halfway through, until meat and bones are browned.

3. Place bones, meat, and carrots in a large stockpot along with drippings and browned bits. Add celery and garlic, then top with cold water, reaching 2" over bones.

4. Cook stock on burner's lowest setting for 4–6 hours. Remove from burner. Discard bones.

5. Using cheesecloth, strain the stock to separate the liquid from the vegetables and meat. Save these solids for another dish, for a stuffable treat toy, or for tasty toppers on your dog's food.

6. Refrigerate the liquid. When cold, the fat will rise to the top of the liquid. Remove and discard this solidified fat. Freeze the stock. It's handy to freeze it in plastic zip-top bags with 1 cup in each or in ice cube trays. Beef Stock makes a flavorful substitute for water or chicken broth in many dog recipes and also is a tasty frozen treat. Refrigerate for up to 3 days or freeze in an airtight container for up to 6 months.

Liver Gravy GF P

A spoonful of this tasty gravy can be a great way to encourage your dog to try new foods—put it on top of the dish you're trying to introduce. Frozen ice cubes also make a great summer treat!

YIELDS: 3–4 cups

1 pound chicken liver, rinsed

1 tablespoon olive oil

2 cups chicken broth

1. In a large skillet over medium-high heat, cook liver in oil until browned.

2. Remove liver from heat and place in a blender. Add chicken broth. Pulse until puréed.

3. Refrigerate for up to 3 days or freeze in an airtight container for up to 6 months.

Turkey Gravy

This easy turkey gravy makes a quick accompaniment to your Thanksgiving meal, but you can also reserve it to prepare for your pooch anytime. As with all gravies, limit servings to just 1 teaspoon as a meal topper.

YIELDS: About 2 cups

2 cups pan drippings

¼ cup all-purpose flour

¼ cup water

1. Remove fat from the drippings by cooling drippings then skimming the fat from the top. Reserve ¼ cup of fat for use in this recipe.

2. In a large skillet, heat the ¼ cup fat and add flour over medium-high heat.

3. Stir constantly for about 1 minute to brown flour. Pour in turkey drippings and water, stirring constantly, and reduce to desired thickness.

4. Cool completely before serving to dogs. Use a spoonful as a meal topper. Refrigerate for up to 3 days or freeze in an airtight container for up to 6 months.

Giblet Gravy

Today, several companies offer commercial gravies to put on your dog's food, but it's easy to make your own healthy gravy from whole foods (and you can make some for yourself, too!). Just pour a spoonful on top of your dog's meal for a tasty tidbit.

YIELDS: About 4 cups

1 tablespoon vegetable oil

Neck and giblets from 1 turkey

1 celery rib, chopped

1 carrot, chopped

4 cups water

2 cups chicken broth

2–3 tablespoons all-purpose flour

1. In a large saucepan, heat oil over medium heat, then add neck and giblets. Brown meat, then add remaining ingredients except flour.

2. Simmer for about 1 hour. Remove from heat.

3. Strain broth through a fine sieve. Skim off and discard fat.

4. Remove meat from bones; discard bones. Finely dice meat.

5. Add meat to broth with flour, stirring while reheating. Bring to a boil, stirring constantly, until gravy thickens.

6. Remove from heat and cool before serving to dogs. Refrigerate for up to 3 days or freeze in an airtight container for up to 6 months.

Chicken Gravy

This simple sauce can be used in many different ways to enhance Rover's mealtime. It can be a tasty topper over kibble, a flavorful addition to a KONG® stuffable treat, or a topper to his commercial meal.

YIELDS: 1 cup

2 tablespoons butter or margarine

2 tablespoons all-purpose flour

1¼ cups Homemade Chicken Broth (see recipe in this chapter)

½ cup milk

1. In a large skillet, melt butter over medium heat. Whisk in flour and cook flour in butter for 1 minute, stirring constantly.

2. Add broth and milk, stirring constantly while mixture thickens (about 2 minutes). Remove from heat.

3. Cool before using 1 teaspoon as a topper over your dog's food. Refrigerate for up to 3 days or freeze in an airtight container for up to 6 months.

Bowser's Bacon Gravy

Although dogs with lactose intolerance can't enjoy this gravy, you and your dog can share this gravy as a special occasion topper for your dog's food.

YIELDS: 1½ cups

6 slices bacon

2 tablespoons all-purpose flour

2 cups milk

1. Fry bacon in a large skillet over medium heat until crisp; remove bacon from pan and break into small bits.

2. Remove all but 2 tablespoons of bacon fat from skillet and discard.

3. Add flour to grease and whisk constantly to lightly cook flour. Pour in milk and continue to whisk as gravy thickens, allowing it to bubble before reducing heat. Add bacon bits and stir. Simmer to desired thickness.

4. Cool before serving 1 spoonful as a topper over your dog's food. Refrigerate for up to 3 days or freeze in an airtight container for up to 6 months.

CHAPTER 16

Aspic and Gelatin

Since the Middle Ages, thickened meat broth has been coaxed into forming aspic from the natural gelatin found in beef, veal, pork, poultry, and even some fish. Before modern refrigeration, it was an ingenious way to protect the dish from spoiling by sealing it off from the air. These savory jellies also made a nice presentation at mealtime. Enthusiasm for the use of aspic and gelatin in human recipes has waned, but you can bet that anything that is meat-derived will appeal to canine taste buds. Your pooches may not appreciate the elegance of an aspic dish, but you'll have fun making this traditional meal for them.

Aspic GF P

Aspic, a savory gelatin, is a time-tested way to prepare vegetable and meat ingredients. Use the aspic in place of broth in recipes, as a low-calorie treat, or as an addition to another meal.

YIELD: 5 cups

2 pounds pigs' feet

Water, as needed

5–8 large chicken drumsticks, thighs, or any cuts with bones

1 large carrot

1 celery rib

2 teaspoons salt

1. Soak pigs' feet in cold water and refrigerate overnight.

2. Place chicken and pigs' feet in a large stockpot and cover with water. Bring to a boil. Remove from stove and discard water.

3. Cover meat with fresh water, with just ½" water over the meat. Cover and bring to a boil, then reduce heat to simmer. Simmer for 5 hours.

4. Add carrot, celery, and salt; simmer for 1 hour.

5. Remove meat and vegetables from broth. Discard pigs' feet and celery rib.

6. Filter broth through sieve.

7. Remove chicken from bones; discard bones. Slice carrots and place in the bottom of a medium bowl. Top with shredded chicken. Slowly pour broth over chicken and carrots, then refrigerate bowl overnight.

8. Set the bowl in hot water for a few seconds, then invert bowl on a plate to remove aspic, using a slim spatula to separate gelatin from bowl if necessary. Refrigerate for up to 3 days or separate into portions and freeze in an airtight container for up to 6 months.

············ **Perk Up Those Tastebuds** ············

Aspic makes a good topper for picky eaters and good stuffing to add to veggies and meat in stuffable treat toys.

Poultry Aspic GF P

Creating an aspic dish is a novel way to add variety to Fido's meal. It makes a nice presentation for special occasions, too, if you prepare the recipe using multiple small bowls the size of your dog's meal.

YIELDS: 5–7 cups

1 whole chicken (about 4 pounds), washed

2 large turkey wings, washed

Water, as needed

2 carrots, cut in 1" pieces

3 celery stalks, cut in 1" pieces

2 cloves garlic (optional)

2 hard-boiled eggs, sliced

1. Remove giblets from chicken and reserve for another recipe.

2. Place chicken and turkey in a large stockpot. Fill with just enough cold water to cover. Cook over medium heat and bring to boil.

3. Skim off fat and foam. Add vegetables and again bring to a boil. Lower heat and simmer for 4 hours.

4. Remove from heat. Remove chicken and turkey, discarding bones and skin. Use two forks to shred meat, reserving it in a container.

5. Strain broth to remove vegetables; reserve those for use in another recipe.

6. Place shredded meat in the bottom of a large bowl. Top with egg slices.

7. Gently pour strained broth over mixture. Refrigerate overnight.

8. To remove aspic from bowl, dip bowl in hot water and invert on a plate, using a slim spatula to separate gelatin from bowl if necessary. Refrigerate for up to 3 days.

Beef Marrow Aspic GF P

Making your own beef stock, jellied as aspic, from marrow bones is inexpensive and easy. You can continue to use the bones to make multiple batches of stock. The stock will begin as a jellied aspic, and as the bones cook down, it will gradually become more liquid as you reach seven or eight days of use.

YIELDS: 2–3 quarts

3 pounds beef marrow bones (beef feet recommended)

2 tablespoons organic apple cider vinegar

3 carrots, chopped in 1" rounds

3 celery sticks, chopped

Water, as needed

1. Place all ingredients in slow cooker and top with enough water to cover 1" over meat. Turn slow cooker on low.

2. After 8–10 hours, use tongs to carefully remove bones. Using a knife, push marrow into the soup. Return bones to pot.

3. Cook on low for 24 hours.

4. Cool broth and strain, using meat and vegetables to add to your dog's meal. Store broth and freeze for later use. Refrigerate for up to 3 days or freeze in an airtight container for up to 6 months. (The refrigeration forms the aspic; because of the long, long cooking time, the minerals and marrow from the bones will leach into the water and create the aspic when refrigerated.)

5. Add water back to bones to make another batch of broth, or discard bones. (Never feed dogs cooked bones; the risk of splintering is much higher in cooked bones.)

A Healthy Dose of Vinegar

The vinegar in this recipe helps to draw minerals from the bones. Although you can use white vinegar, apple cider vinegar is tastier to your dog and also has many health benefits. Many dog lovers add a teaspoon to their dog's food two or three times a week to help with tear stains, skin irritations, rashes, and more.

Jellied Chicken Salad GF P

Humans usually consider chicken salad a side dish, but it can also be a cool meal for your pooches. It's especially welcome during warmer weather.

YIELDS: 4 cups

1¾ cups Homemade Chicken Broth (see Chapter 15), divided

1 envelope unflavored gelatin

2 cups chopped cooked chicken

¼ cup chopped celery

1. Pour ½ cup of chicken broth in a saucepan over medium heat. Pour gelatin in chicken broth, stirring to completely dissolve. Add remainder of chicken broth and continue to stir to mix.

2. Stir in chicken and celery, then pour into a large bowl or loaf pan.

3. Refrigerate overnight, or at least 12 hours.

4. To remove, dip bowl in hot water and use a thin spatula to separate the salad from the bowl as you invert it over a plate. Refrigerate for up to 3 days or freeze in an airtight container for up to 6 months.

STANDARD U.S./METRIC CONVERSION CHART

VOLUME CONVERSIONS

U.S. Volume Measure	Metric Equivalent
⅛ teaspoon	0.5 milliliter
¼ teaspoon	1 milliliter
½ teaspoon	2 milliliters
1 teaspoon	5 milliliters
½ tablespoon	7 milliliters
1 tablespoon (3 teaspoons)	15 milliliters
2 tablespoons (1 fluid ounce)	30 milliliters
¼ cup (4 tablespoons)	60 milliliters
⅓ cup	90 milliliters
½ cup (4 fluid ounces)	125 milliliters
⅔ cup	160 milliliters
¾ cup (6 fluid ounces)	180 milliliters
1 cup (16 tablespoons)	250 milliliters
1 pint (2 cups)	500 milliliters
1 quart (4 cups)	1 liter (about)

WEIGHT CONVERSIONS

U.S. Weight Measure	Metric Equivalent
½ ounce	15 grams
1 ounce	30 grams
2 ounces	60 grams
3 ounces	85 grams
¼ pound (4 ounces)	115 grams
½ pound (8 ounces)	225 grams
¾ pound (12 ounces)	340 grams
1 pound (16 ounces)	454 grams

OVEN TEMPERATURE CONVERSIONS

Degrees Fahrenheit	Degrees Celsius
200 degrees F	95 degrees C
250 degrees F	120 degrees C
275 degrees F	135 degrees C
300 degrees F	150 degrees C
325 degrees F	160 degrees C
350 degrees F	180 degrees C
375 degrees F	190 degrees C
400 degrees F	205 degrees C
425 degrees F	220 degrees C
450 degrees F	230 degrees C

BAKING PAN SIZES

U.S.	Metric
8 × 1½ inch round baking pan	20 × 4 cm cake tin
9 × 1½ inch round baking pan	23 × 3.5 cm cake tin
11 × 7 × 1½ inch baking pan	28 × 18 × 4 cm baking tin
13 × 9 × 2 inch baking pan	30 × 20 × 5 cm baking tin
2 quart rectangular baking dish	30 × 20 × 3 cm baking tin
15 × 10 × 2 inch baking pan	30 × 25 × 2 cm baking tin (Swiss roll tin)
9 inch pie plate	22 × 4 or 23 × 4 cm pie plate
7 or 8 inch springform pan	18 or 20 cm springform or loose bottom cake tin
9 × 5 × 3 inch loaf pan	23 × 13 × 7 cm or 2 lb narrow loaf or pâté tin
1½ quart casserole	1.5 liter casserole
2 quart casserole	2 liter casserole

Index